Jobs for the Hard-to-Employ

New Directions
for a Public-Private
Partnership

Jobs for the Hard-to-Employ:
New Directions for a Public-Private Partnership

Related Materials

Please write to CED for information on other publications and materials on jobs for the hard-to-employ:

"Training and Jobs Programs in Action: Case Studies in Private-Sector Initiatives for the Hard-to-Employ"

> Presents the results of a CED survey of what over 60 companies and organizations are doing to develop training and jobs for the hard-to-employ.

Review and Discussion Guide: "Jobs for the Hard-to-Employ"

> Designed to stimulate discussion and debate on the issues raised in this CED policy statement.

Digest: "Jobs for the Hard-to-Employ"

> A pocket-size summary of the key issues and major recommendations contained in this CED policy statement.

Filmstrip: "Jobs for the Hard-to-Employ"

> A 14-minute color filmstrip with synchronized sound track explaining key issues covered in this CED policy statement.

Committee for Economic Development
477 Madison Avenue, New York, N.Y. 10022 (212) 688-2063

Jobs for the Hard-to-Employ

New Directions
for a Public-Private
Partnership

A Statement on National Policy
by the Research and Policy Committee
of the Committee for Economic Development

January 1978

Library of Congress Cataloging in Publication Data

 Committee for Economic Development.
  Jobs for the hard-to-employ.

   1. Hard-core unemployed—United States.
2. Manpower policy—United States. 3. Occupational
training—United States. I. Title.
HD5724.C6647 1978 331.1'1'0973 77-28272
ISBN 0-87186-766-4 lib. bdg.
ISBN 0-87186-066-X pbk.

First printing: January 1978
Paperbound: $3.00
Library binding: $4.50
Printed in the United States of America by Georgian Press, Inc.
Design: Harry Carter

COMMITTEE FOR ECONOMIC DEVELOPMENT
477 Madison Avenue, New York, N.Y. 10022
1700 K Street, N.W., Washington, D.C. 20006

Contents

4

The Research and Policy Committee is not attempting to pass judgment on any pending specific legislative proposals; its purpose is to urge careful consideration of the objectives set forth in this statement and of the best means of accomplishing those objectives.

Each statement on national policy is preceded by discussions, meetings, and exchanges of memoranda, often stretching over many months. The research is undertaken by a subcommittee, assisted by advisors chosen for their competence in the field under study. The members and advisors of the subcommittee that prepared this statement are listed on page 6.

The full Research and Policy Committee participates in the drafting of findings and recommendations. Likewise, the trustees on the drafting subcommittee vote to approve or disapprove a policy statement, and they share with the Research and Policy Committee the privilege of submitting individual comments for publication, as noted on this and the following page and on the appropriate page of the text of the statement.

Except for the members of the Research and Policy Committee and the responsible subcommittee, the recommendations presented herein are not necessarily endorsed by other trustees or by the advisors, contributors, staff members, or others associated with CED.

6

Purpose
of This Statement

TEN YEARS AGO, AT A TIME OF GREAT TROUBLE in many urban areas, there was a strong outpouring of business commitment to bring jobs and businesses back to the central city. However, in many cases, these commitments were made without an understanding of the problems involved and without the experience necessary to develop effective programs. As a result, many of the efforts failed. Many business leaders concluded that there was really very little they could do that would be effective and lasting. It became, in their minds, primarily a problem for government.

However, some business groups continued to work at the problems of the hard-to-employ and began to gain experience and deeper understanding. In the past two years, there has been a renewal of business's commitment to developing jobs for the hard-to-employ and for helping prepare the disadvantaged, particularly minority youths, for steady, responsible jobs. What makes current efforts different from those of the 1960s is that now there is a realization of the difficulties involved and an understanding of the effort that must be put into each job and into preparing each individual for that job.

The CED Subcommittee that prepared this report spent two years examining what kinds of programs have worked, what kinds have not, and why. In cooperation with the Work in America Institute, CED has conducted a survey of its own trustee companies and other firms that are carrying out many of the types of efforts called for in this statement. The

7

results of that survey are contained in *Training and Jobs Programs in Action: Case Studies in Private-Sector Initiatives for the Hard-to-Employ*, which is being issued as a companion to this statement.

Achieving high employment has long been a national goal. But after more than two years of recovery from the nation's worst postwar recession, unemployment rates remain distressingly high.

Over the years, the basic response to high unemployment has been to develop a set of fiscal and monetary policies that can promote a vigorous and sustained demand expansion without causing undue inflation. Yet, both business and government are coming to realize that although fiscal and monetary policies and other sound economic policies are essential, special measures are needed to deal with the growing problem of structural unemployment—the kind of unemployment that even in the best of times affects the undereducated, the unskilled, and those who are considered too young or too old or who are subject to discrimination.

This statement by the CED Research and Policy Committee focuses on ways of overcoming unemployment and underemployment for those groups that typically experience high or prolonged joblessness. From the beginning of this project, we have felt that finding ways to deal with structural unemployment is vital to achieving the longer-term goal of high employment without inflation.

A Practical Approach. One of our major conclusions was that unemployment and underemployment are costly both to society and to the economy. Therefore, we believe that the kind of steps we recommend are not only good social policy but also good business. In addition, we agreed that the principal stress of public policy should be on developing productive jobs rather than on paying people for not working.

Although there is an important role for government in the employment picture, it is the private sector that provides most of the jobs in the American economy. Therefore, the statement calls for increased training and job opportunities in the private sector and stepped-up transition of the hard-to-employ from government income support and subsidized jobs into permanent private employment.

Expanded private-sector efforts should not be limited to large corporate employers but should take advantage of the many opportunities to be found among small businesses.

New Directions for the Private Sector. Both business and government have gained valuable lessons from the training and jobs efforts of the last decade. During the 1960s, many programs were hastily conceived —often in response to various forms of social unrest. The country has now moved beyond this crisis atmosphere, and there are already many private-sector programs throughout the country that are meeting the needs of both business and the hard-to-employ.

The Importance of Work. The Subcommittee that prepared this policy statement was also concerned with a concept of work that goes beyond simply being a source of income. Work and the work ethic have intrinsic benefits—to the individual and to society. Work provides a point of identification, a source of self-esteem, and a vital part of most people's systems of values.

Because of the importance of work, we were also concerned with the social and economic consequences of separating millions of people from productive jobs. In addition to the personal desperation and frustration that stem from unemployment, there are major economic costs in terms of lost output, waste of human and capital resources, and support of an ever increasing number of nonworkers.

Although no firm should be asked to make special efforts if it would jeopardize its efficiency, we see several strong indications that both business and society will benefit from an increased private-sector commitment to training and hiring the hard-to-employ.

As the economy grows, there will be an increasing need for skilled workers. This need will be even greater if, as population trends suggest, the percentage of young people in the work force grows more slowly than in the past.

There is also a growing awareness on the part of government that the private sector should play a larger training and employment role, and there is a growing concern over the inflationary impact of broadening the scope of public-sector programs.

No one policy or set of programs will work for all businesses. What is needed instead are increased options and incentives for businesses, unions, and profit and nonprofit organizations to enlarge employment and training programs for groups that face special difficulties.

Acknowledgments. The CED Subcommittee that prepared this statement brought together an extraordinary range of talents, interests, and experience. A list of Subcommittee members and advisors appears on page 6. The Subcommittee benefited greatly from the skilled and persuasive leadership of its chairman, John L. Burns, former president of

10

RCA and former board chairman and chief executive officer of Cities Service Company.

We also wish to extend special thanks to project director Frank W. Schiff, vice president and chief economist of CED, for providing a clear and incisive approach to this complex issue and to associate project directors Owen C. Johnson, Jerome M. Rosow, and Harold L. Sheppard.

We are indebted to the Edna McConnell Clark Foundation for the generous support that has allowed us to produce this statement. We are especially grateful for the foundation's support of a program of information and education activities that will enable CED to conduct a series of policy forums on this subject in areas of the country where structural unemployment is especially severe.

Franklin A. Lindsay, *Chairman*
Research and Policy Committee

Chapter 1
Introduction and Summary
of Major Recommendations

AMERICANS HAVE LONG CONSIDERED it a basic goal to have the opportunity to work, to earn a decent living, and to provide for their families. For the vast majority of adults, what they do to earn that living constitutes a vital part of their identity and sense of values.

Yet, the United States has within its population a growing number of people with special burdens that keep them out of the mainstream of the labor force. Most jobs in this country are designed for prime-age, full-time, socially disciplined workers. However, there are large groups of people in this country who want to work but cannot obtain useful jobs, even in relatively good times, because they

- are undereducated, unskilled, or inexperienced
- are considered too young or too old
- are unable to work full time
- are subject to discrimination or restrictive labor market practices
- lack the basic work disciplines and abilities necessary to get and hold a steady job

11

For the past thirty years, high employment has been a major goal of the nation's economic policy. But except during wartime, this goal has rarely been achieved. During recent years, in fact, the official unemployment rate reached its highest level since the Great Depression. In the first eleven months of 1977, the average number of unemployed still amounted to 6.9 million persons, or 7.1 percent of the civilian labor force.

We believe that this country must make a strong national commitment to high employment and to a situation in which the number of job openings essentially matches the number of those seeking jobs at reasonable wages and in which people able and willing to work have adequate opportunities to be trained and guided toward suitable job vacancies within a reasonable period of time. This commitment must, of course, be pursued in a manner consistent with the nation's other major economic and social objectives, especially the need to curtail inflation.

The primary means of developing adequate training and job opportunities is through strengthening the demand for goods and services in the economy as a whole and in particular sectors and regions.*

A vigorous and sustained demand expansion is necessary to overcome *cyclical* joblessness (which stems primarily from an overall deficiency in demand). It is also the single most effective means of reducing *structural unemployment,* which affects particular groups of job seekers because their education, skills, or locations do not readily match available jobs or because they are handicapped by discrimination and other labor market barriers. However, experience has shown that by itself, a demand expansion strong enough to result in a dramatic rise in jobs for the hard-to-employ is also likely to create serious inflationary pressures.

But the tasks of achieving sustained high employment and conquering inflation are not mutually exclusive. They can and must be attacked simultaneously. Therefore, any steps toward healthy demand expansion need to be accompanied by a range of measures to make the economy less inflation-prone. These should include steps to increase its competitiveness and efficiency, to eliminate restrictive practices in product and labor markets, and to enlarge capacity and supply availability.

In earlier policy statements, CED has dealt extensively with ways to improve overall demand management, strengthen economic efficiency and investment incentives, and fight inflation. We are continuing active studies in all these areas. In addition, our new study *Revitalizing America's Cities* is examining the massive problems of the nation's urban centers, including the plight of the deteriorated inner cities, where unemployment is highest. We will explore ways to create the conditions that might bring needed

*See memorandum by R. STEWART RAUCH, JR., page 88.

jobs back to these areas and, where necessary, to help bring inner-city residents to suitable jobs in other locations. In other studies, we shall examine means of averting or overcoming the special unemployment problems caused by such factors as unfair foreign trade competition and excessive government regulation.

In this policy statement, we are concerned primarily with the urgent need for a wide variety of measures to cope *directly* with the structural unemployment problems of those groups that have consistently had special difficulties in the labor market—particularly the young, the old, and the disadvantaged—and to increase incentives for productive work.

Unfortunately, there is no single solution or major policy program that can eliminate unemployment for all these chronically affected groups. What is needed instead is an integrated set of public and private actions that will benefit groups and areas of the economy with particularly severe unemployment problems without aggravating the existing inflation.

Government programs to train and provide jobs for the hard-to-employ, including public-service employment, must continue to play a major role in national manpower policy.* We welcome the recent increased emphasis by both Congress and the Administration on direct measures to deal with the unemployment problems of hard-hit groups, particularly disadvantaged youths and veterans.

However, four out of five jobs in the United States are in the private sector. A stronger private-public partnership must be developed to increase training and job opportunities in that sector and to speed the transition of the hard-to-employ from government income support and subsidized public or private jobs to permanent private employment. Key ways in which this can best be accomplished are the focus of this study. In particular, we recommend the following measures:

● **New and expanded use on a nationwide basis of private-sector programs that already work effectively and creation of a clearinghouse for disseminating information about successful and innovative programs** (see Chapter 4)

● **Stronger organizational mechanisms to mobilize private-sector involvement** (see Chapter 4), including much wider use of

—direct government manpower contracts with private nonprofit organizations created by consortia of business firms

14

—other types of intermediary organizations that can help business handle job development, training, and placement activities
—jobs corporations to provide training and jobs for the hardest-to-employ
—cooperative community efforts, involving businesses, nonprofit organizations, unions, schools, and governments, to increase training and job opportunities

● **Increased incentives and reduced disincentives for private employment of the hard-to-employ,** including additional experimentation with categorical tax credits, with stipends for trainees and apprentices, and with selective exemptions from the minimum wage and increased social security earnings ceilings (see Chapter 4)

● **Improved approaches to the problems of particular groups among the hard-to-employ** (see Chapter 5), including

—increased stress on business involvement in skill training and upgrading of the disadvantaged
—an improved transition from school to work for youths as well as other age-groups, including increased use of apprenticeship and cooperative education programs
—more productive use of midcareer and older workers, including steps to smooth the transition from regular work to retirement
—increased and wider use of alternative work patterns to make more employment available to the young, the old, and other workers who cannot conform to a full-time work schedule

● **Greater business use of alternatives to outright layoffs in recessions,** including skill upgrading and work sharing (see Chapter 5)

● **Improved management and closer integration of government programs that facilitate the employment of the hard-to-employ,** particularly the U.S. Employment Service and the Comprehensive Employment and Training Act (CETA) programs (see Chapter 6)

This agenda for action is neither impractical nor visionary. In fact, many businesses, nonprofit organizations, and governments throughout the country are currently carrying out many such programs that are increasing training and job opportunities for the hard-to-employ. In connection with this policy statement, CED has surveyed its own trustees' companies and other firms and has found numerous instances of successful private-sector programs and constructive business-government cooperation. Examples of these programs are cited in Chapters 4 and 5. We will publish fuller descriptions of close to sixty private-sector programs in a companion volume of case studies.

These and other successful programs can and should serve as models for more action and innovation by both large and small businesses and for more active business-government-community cooperation. Focusing attention on these programs should also help government agencies and civil servants to be more receptive to such initiatives.

To be fully effective, the approaches that we recommend in this statement must be paralleled by continuing strong efforts to overcome the barriers to employment and career advancement that are the result of discrimination. For example, even the best skill-training program for the hard-to-employ is of little use if those who complete it are refused jobs because of their race, sex, or age. There is also a major need for identifying and changing various existing legislative requirements, government regulations, and union or business practices that tend to discourage employment of the disadvantaged and other hard-to-employ groups.*

There have been suggestions that the nation can learn to live with unemployment and can simply give income support to those who are poorly equipped to compete for available jobs. However, we believe that this country cannot justifiably deny its citizens the opportunity to work for an adequate income and to be free from the desperation and frustration that frequent or long-term unemployment can bring. Nor can the country ignore the huge economic and social costs of goods not produced and services not rendered and the truly enormous costs of supporting an increasing number of nonworkers. In the long term, such wasteful use of resources is likely to add to rather than curtail inflation.

Both government and business must acknowledge these costs and begin to break down the barriers that separate millions of people from productive work. In doing so, they will find, we believe, that most people want to work, that most of the unemployed are employable, and that most of the untrained are trainable.

*See memorandum by JAMES Q. RIORDAN, page 89.

Chapter 2
The Dimensions and
Costs of Unemployment

To MANY PEOPLE, it seems paradoxical that this country is experiencing high and continuous unemployment at a time when the total number of jobs is increasing at near-record rates and when in various areas and occupations the number of job vacancies apparently exceeds the number of job seekers. The fact is that today's unemployment is not the result of an absolute reduction in the total number of jobs, as had been true during the recent business downturn. Indeed, the proportion of Americans working today is actually somewhat higher than it was a decade ago. But the number of persons seeking work has risen even faster than the number of available jobs over the decade, and the rate of unemployment is now almost double what it was ten years ago (see Figure 1, page 19, and "The Changing Character of the Labor Force," page 20).

Why is it so difficult to attain high employment? One reason is that the traditional remedy of creating jobs by expanding total demand through fiscal and monetary policies cannot be pushed beyond a certain point without creating serious inflationary pressures. Such inflation would not only be harmful by itself but could also serve to worsen the unemployment problem. Equally important, however, is the fact that traditional

16

remedies alone cannot adequately resolve the unemployment problems of many groups that typically experience unusually high or prolonged levels of joblessness: the young, the old, and the disadvantaged, especially blacks and members of other minority groups living in inner cities.

WHO ARE THE UNEMPLOYED?

On average, 7.3 million persons, or 7.7 percent of the civilian labor force, were out of work during each month of 1976. Over 20 million persons experienced unemployment sometime during the year. Many were jobless for a relatively short time; close to 40 percent were unemployed for less than five weeks. However, 32 percent of the total suffered extended periods of joblessness (fifteen weeks or more), compared with 24 percent in 1972.

The official unemployment totals provide only a partial indication of the real extent of unemployment. Not counted in the overall number for 1976 were 910,000 discouraged workers who wanted a job but were not looking for one because they believed that none was available. It is also noteworthy that in 1975 over 4 million persons were employed full time but their income remained below the poverty level.

Heads of households, the group that the public usually associates with high unemployment, constituted less than 40 percent of the total unemployed in 1976. The 5.1 percent unemployment rate for this group was far lower than the national average.

For some groups and regions, however, unemployment has typically been much higher than for others (see Figures 2 and 3, pages 21 and 23, and Table 1 of the Appendix).

- Young people (16 to 24 years of age) accounted for close to half of the total unemployed in 1976, even though they constituted less than a quarter of the labor force. The unemployment rate for 16- to 19-year-olds was 19 percent; for 20- to 24-year-olds, it was 12 percent.

- The 1976 unemployment rate for nonwhites (13.1 percent) was almost twice as high as that for whites (7 percent), roughly the same differential that has prevailed for over two decades.

- Less educated workers and those with limited skills suffered particularly high rates of unemployment. High school dropouts had an unemployment rate of 32.9 percent in 1975. In some inner cities, the

Figure 1. Although the employed proportion of the U.S. population is higher today than it was ten years ago, the unemployment rate has almost doubled, as the number of persons looking for work has risen much faster than the number of available jobs.

unemployment rate for dropouts was reported to be as high as 60 percent.

- The unemployment rate in 1976 for adult women (7.4 percent) was significantly higher than that for adult men (5.9 percent).

- Unemployment was far higher in some cities and areas than in others. In 1976, the central cities of Detroit and Saint Louis had unemployment rates of 13.1 percent and 12.8 percent, respectively, compared with the national average of 7.7 percent.

Although the unemployment rates for older workers were lower than the average, these workers tended to be out of work for a much longer time (see Figure 4, page 25). Also—and this is not adequately reflected in the statistics—a significant number of older workers would like to work but have been pressed into early retirement. Moreover, the number of discouraged workers among both older workers and nonwhites tends to be particularly high.

Unemployment problems are multiplied when a person belongs to more than one high-unemployment-risk category. Unemployment among black teen-agers was close to 40 percent in 1976, and the percentage was even higher for black teen-agers living in inner cities.

A major factor complicating the U.S. unemployment problem is the presence and continuing inflow of a large number of illegal immigrants. Estimates of the number of illegal aliens in this country vary greatly, but the total clearly comes to several million. Some recent estimates have placed it at over 8 million.[1] Illegal aliens are often in direct competition

---

1./ For more detailed discussions, see National Council on Employment Policy, *Illegal Aliens: An Assessment of the Issues* (October 1976), and Economic Development Council of New York, *The Illegal Alien and the Economy* (April 1977).

Employment-Population Ratio and Unemployment Rate, 1956 to 1977

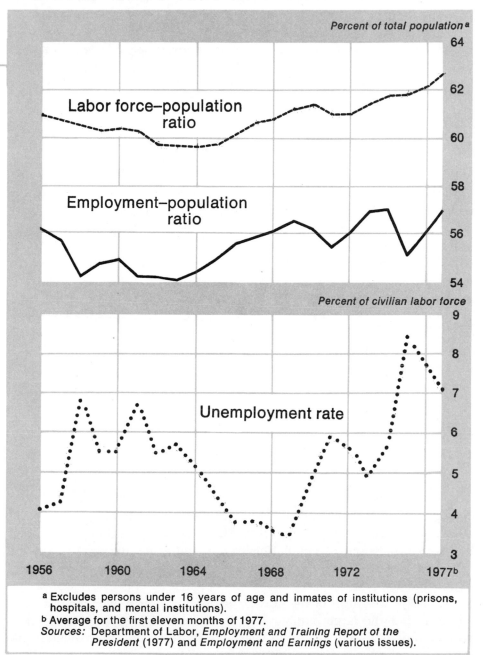

Percent of total population [a]

Labor force–population ratio

Employment–population ratio

Percent of civilian labor force

Unemployment rate

1956   1960   1964   1968   1972   1977 [b]

[a] Excludes persons under 16 years of age and inmates of institutions (prisons, hospitals, and mental institutions).

[b] Average for the first eleven months of 1977.

Sources: Department of Labor, *Employment and Training Report of the President* (1977) and *Employment and Earnings* (various issues).

19

Figure 2. For some groups, unemployment in the last twenty years has consistently been much higher than it has for others—in good times as well as bad. The unemployment rate for white teen-agers has remained three to four times as high as the rate for male adults, and the unemployment rate for black teen-agers has been approximately double the rate for white teen-agers. The jobless rate for adult women has also been persistently higher than that for adult males.

with the most disadvantaged groups in the regular U.S. labor force for unskilled and low-skill jobs. Partly because of their illegal status, many are willing to accept working conditions and pay not acceptable to legal residents, and employers hiring illegals can often avoid payment of payroll taxes for such workers.

In our view, the illegal alien problem and its relation to unemployment have by now reached such serious proportions that they call for priority attention and action by both government and the private sector. **We urge that a major effort be undertaken promptly to obtain more accurate information regarding the size of the illegal alien problem and to develop remedial steps, such as use of universal social security cards and stronger penalties for employers who knowingly hire illegal aliens.***

THE CHANGING CHARACTER OF THE LABOR FORCE

Future employment strategies must take careful account of the changing character of the labor force during the next ten to fifteen years. (See Appendix, Tables 2, 3, and 4 for the latest Census–Bureau of Labor Statistics projections of population trends and labor force participation rates and the resultant percent distribution of the labor force according to age and sex.)

Nearly two-thirds of the growth of the labor force over the last decade reflected the large number of women and youths entering the job market. For example, 16- to 24-year-olds represented approximately 24 percent of the labor force in 1976, compared with 17 percent in 1960.

*See memorandum by W. D. EBERLE, page 89.

Unemployment Rate, by Age and Sex, 1956 to 1977

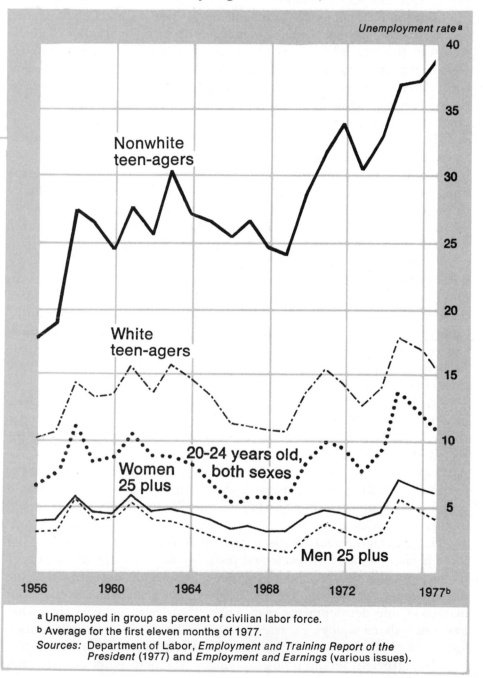

Unemployment rate [a]

- Nonwhite teen-agers
- White teen-agers
- 20-24 years old, both sexes
- Women 25 plus
- Men 25 plus

1956 1960 1964 1968 1972 1977[b]

[a] Unemployed in group as percent of civilian labor force.
[b] Average for the first eleven months of 1977.

Sources: Department of Labor, *Employment and Training Report of the President* (1977) and *Employment and Earnings* (various issues).

Moreover, women constituted 40 percent of the labor force in 1976, compared with 33 percent in 1960.

But this does not mean (as is often mistakenly assumed) that women and teen-agers account for most of the recent *rise* in joblessness. On the contrary, the increase in unemployment associated with the recent recession was most pronounced among adult men and heads of families. Although unemployment rates for these groups are still far higher than at the prerecession peak, these are also the groups that will be more readily absorbed into the work force as the recovery progresses.

In the next ten to fifteen years, labor force growth will be concentrated in the prime age-groups, as persons born during the postwar baby boom move from their teens into their twenties. Thus, although the importance of teen-agers in the labor force will decline only gradually through 1980, it will fall in both percentage and absolute terms by 1990, when they will represent only 6.7 percent of the labor force, compared with 9.5 percent in 1976.

A second major trend will be a continued upturn in the labor force participation of women. According to the projections issued by the Bureau of Labor Statistics in December 1976, the rate of female labor force participation can be expected to increase from 47 percent in 1976 to 52 percent by 1990. In recent months, the rise in this rate has substantially exceeded the projected trend, and it seems quite possible that female participation rates will prove to be considerably higher by 1980 and 1990 than current official projections indicate.

A third factor will be the changing role of older workers. The share of persons aged 65 and over in the total population will continue to rise through 1990. Partly because of the trend toward early retirement, the recent Bureau of Labor Statistics projections indicated that labor force participation rates of workers 55 and older will decline significantly, particularly among men. However, the pending legislation that would prohibit mandatory retirement before age 70 for most workers could modify this projected decline.

In general, current trends suggest that the coming decade's labor force is likely to be more stable and probably more productive because a larger percentage of the total labor force will become concentrated in the prime age-groups, which have relatively regular attachment to the labor market. These developments may make it easier to achieve somewhat lower overall unemployment rates with given levels of capacity utilization and rates of economic expansion than has been the case in recent years.

Nevertheless, serious problems remain. The percentage of teen-agers

Figure 3: Unemployment Rate, by Race, 1956 to 1977

Nonwhite percent of
civilian labor force

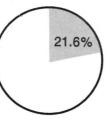

Nonwhite percent of
total unemployment

Although black workers
currently make up
11.6 percent of the labor
force, they account
for 21.6 percent of
the unemployed.

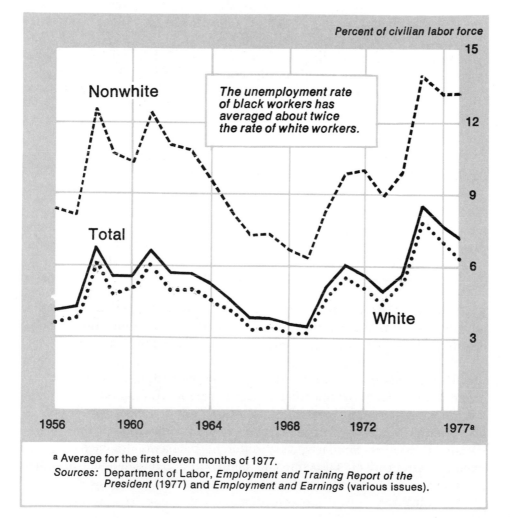

Percent of civilian labor force

Nonwhite

*The unemployment rate
of black workers has
averaged about twice
the rate of white workers.*

Total

White

1956   1960   1964   1968   1972   1977ª

a Average for the first eleven months of 1977.

Sources: Department of Labor, *Employment and Training Report of the
President* (1977) and *Employment and Earnings* (various issues).

Figure 4. Older workers have lower overall rates of recorded unemployment than other age-groups. However, they include a higher percentage of persons who want a job but who are not counted as unemployed because they are too discouraged to look for work. Furthermore, when older workers become unemployed, they tend to remain jobless longer than other age-groups.

in the economy is not expected to drop significantly during the remainder of the decade, and projections indicate that the percentage of nonwhite teen-agers will not drop at all during the next ten years. At the same time, the fact that after 1980 there will be fewer young entrants into the labor force increases the possibility of future shortages of skilled workers. These statistics also raise troubling questions about whether this society may seriously underutilize the productive resources represented by older workers.

THE COSTS OF UNEMPLOYMENT: HOW SERIOUS?

Although there is a widespread consensus that current unemployment levels are too high, there are different views of how severe unemployment is and by how much it can and should be reduced. However, the full costs of unemployment, not only to the individuals affected but to all sectors of the economy and society, are often not taken into account.

Economic Hardship. For many, joblessness means serious hardships and deprivation, not only in terms of forgone income but also in terms of lost skills, self-respect, and general physical and emotional well-being.

However, the degree of hardship caused by unemployment can vary widely. For example, there is a difference between the hardships experienced by an unemployed worker who is permanently laid off and by one who expects to be recalled within a relatively short period, particularly if his income is almost fully protected by regular and supplemental unemployment benefits. Similarly, very different problems are faced by the unemployed head of a low-income family and by teen-agers or other secondary wage earners, particularly those from families with above-average incomes.

Characteristics of Older Unemployed Workers, 1976

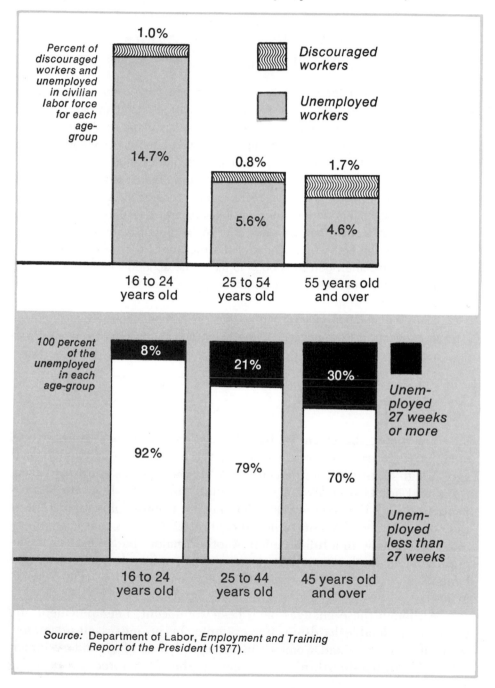

Source: Department of Labor, *Employment and Training Report of the President* (1977).

25

THE UNEVEN RECOVERY
AND THE PROBLEM OF BLACK UNEMPLOYMENT

A striking feature of the economic recovery since the recession trough of March 1975 is that the net reduction in unemployment has been largely due to reemployment of experienced workers in the prime age-groups. For these workers, unemployment had been cut by about one-half by mid-1977. In contrast, there has been little net change in unemployment levels for new entrants or reentrants into the labor force (primarily teen-agers and women). Moreover, reemployment has been lagging for laid-off minority members and workers over 40. In previous periods of upswing, new entrants and other marginal labor force groups were also usually by-passed in the first several years of the recovery (or at least until the expansion became vigorous enough to move the economy closer to capacity levels). But this pattern seems to be more pronounced in the current expansion.

The situation is most serious for black Americans, especially black teen-agers. In November 1977, the black unemployment rate of 13.8 percent was only about ½ percentage point below its 1975 recession peak;

For many, the extent of hardship associated with a given overall unemployment rate today is less severe than it was ten or twenty years ago. A significantly higher percentage of the labor force consists of teen-agers and adults from two-income families, many of whom are less dependent on full-time employment than heads of households. In fact, more than one-half of today's unemployed come from families that have one or more members with a full-time job. Another major change is the marked improvement in the amount and coverage of unemployment insurance benefits and the dramatic rise in federal income-security transfer payments.

Although these changes have been significant, unemployment still causes considerable hardship. For example, by no means all unemployment of teen-agers and women can be regarded as of secondary importance. About one-fourth of the women in the labor force are heads of

whereas the white unemployment rate (6 percent) was more than 2 percentage points below its record 1975 high. Black teen-age unemployment stood at 39.0 percent, compared with white teen-age joblessness of 14.5 percent. This also constituted a widening of the black-white unemployment gap since 1975. A number of factors contributed to these developments: The working-age black population is expanding at a much more rapid pace than the comparable white population. As economic conditions have improved, many blacks who had previously been too discouraged to look for work have started to enter the labor market. Black employment has grown much more slowly than white employment.

In part, this slower employment growth reflects the fact that the largest employment gains in the current recovery have been in industries with a low concentration of black workers. More fundamentally, the disproportionate share of blacks among the unemployed can in large part be traced to the effects of current and past discrimination. As a September 1977 Labor Department study showed, it also reflects the related high concentration of black workers in central cities, where suitable jobs are often unavailable; their disproportionate representation in the nation's poverty areas; their generally lower levels of educational attainment; and their overrepresentation in low-paying, less-skilled jobs.

households, and for many families, regular paychecks for both husband and wife have become a matter of necessity if the family is to maintain its standard of living, particularly at the current high rates of inflation. In coming years, furthermore, more and more women are likely to view regular employment as a basic part of their way of life. In the case of teenagers, it is noteworthy that a sizable proportion of 18- and 19-year-olds is no longer in school. Failure to absorb these youths into productive employment within a reasonable time can do permanent harm to their long-term job prospects. Moreover, for many young people who are still in school, part-time work is often essential to their remaining in school.

A closer look at the unemployment statistics suggests that many of the real hardship cases are concentrated among poor blacks and other low-income families living in inner cities and among those elements in the youth and older populations who have the greatest difficulty coping with work. It is striking that the share of discouraged workers is particularly high among these groups. For example, inclusion of discouraged workers would almost double the unofficial unemployment rate for all nonwhite men and would triple the rate for nonwhite men between the ages of 45 and 54. Among teen-agers, the most serious problems of unemployment are concentrated among lower-income, out-of-school youths who have been jobless for fifteen weeks or more.

Social and Human Costs. Statistics on income losses by no means tell the full story of the human and social damage that frequent or prolonged unemployment can impose. Many of these costs are indirect and may be felt only after considerable delay. Nevertheless, they are very real.

A recent study conducted at the Johns Hopkins School of Hygiene and Public Health shows a strong correlation between higher unemployment rates and increases in mental disorders, heart diseases, alcoholism, homicide rates, and suicide among adults and in infant and maternal mortality. There is also a positive correlation between the rate of unemployment and applications for disability benefits under social security. Although many of the medical problems resulting from increased unemployment can be traced to the stress, uncertainty, and despair of prolonged joblessness, there are also direct effects. For example, because of the loss of medical insurance benefits, unemployed persons tend to postpone the use of health services, which can lead to increased disabilities.

For some groups, prolonged or frequent unemployment can also lead to alienation from many of the values that are basic to the mainstream of American society, including belief in the work ethic and the importance of a regular day's work. This problem is especially serious for many unemployed youths, particularly disadvantaged teen-agers in deteriorated inner cities who have dropped out of school. Such youths may spend all their formative years in a setting in which regular jobs are not readily available and in which many of those with whom they come in contact live in a nonwork environment.

Older workers are also seriously affected by high unemployment. This may seem surprising because average unemployment rates are lower for older age-groups than for younger ones. But as we have noted, the duration of unemployment tends to be greater for older workers, and they make up a disproportionate share of the discouraged-worker category.

Of course, the unemployment problems of teen-agers and older workers are not necessarily separate. When older workers become unemployed, their teen-age children may be forced to leave school to seek a job.

MEASURING HARDSHIP

There is no regular official index that can be used to measure the degree of hardship associated with unemployment. However, one attempt to construct this kind of measurement has been made by Sar Levitan and Robert Taggart, who have proposed the use of the Employment and Earnings Inadequacy Index (EEI). This index initially includes all persons now covered in the unemployment total and those wanting a job but not actively seeking work because they believe they cannot find it, persons working part time but looking for full-time work, and those employed family heads and single persons not living with families whose earnings for the previous year have been below the poverty level. The index then excludes from the total those groups among the unemployed that can be assumed to encompass many people who are not suffering hardship, including all unemployed persons 65 or older, all those under 22 who are going to school, and all individuals who are members of families earning more than the median income. These exclusions are, of course, somewhat arbitrary and are likely to be on the high side. For example, by no means all unemployed persons 65 or older are without hardship. Using this approach, the index shows that in 1975, 13 percent of the labor force was suffering hardship from unemployment or low incomes, compared with the official unemployment rate of 9.1 percent.

Comparable figures are not available for significantly earlier periods. Therefore, the index does not necessarily alter the conclusion that the degree of hardship associated with a given total unemployment figure may have lessened over the past ten to twenty years. However, the index does suggest that the extent of hardship stemming from the combined effects of unemployment and low incomes is still very substantial; it may, in fact, be greater than the official unemployment statistics alone suggest. Moreover, the index highlights the special severity of unemployment and low earnings for nonwhite families. Thus, for black female heads of households, the Employment and Earnings Inadequacy Index amounted to a staggering 56 percent.

Waste of Resources. Even when the potential hardships of unemployment are alleviated by various forms of income maintenance, society suffers a loss in terms of the goods and services that persons who are out of work or underemployed could have produced if they had been adequately employed. Other costs to society arise from a decline of skills and self-confidence through long-term unemployment, the loss of tax revenues that would otherwise have resulted from higher output, and the expense of supporting the unemployed. In addition, society suffers major losses in terms of budgetary outlays and deterioration in the quality of life as it tries to cope with the costs imposed by higher levels of crime, illness, alcoholism, family breakup, child abuse, and other social burdens and disorders.

One type of cost involves the loss of output of goods and services when the economy operates below high-employment levels. In the recession year 1975, this loss is estimated to have amounted to about $140 billion (in 1972 dollars) if high employment is associated with an unemployment rate of 5 percent. Also added to this cost in terms of forgone output should be the costs of reduced training and deteriorated skills that are consequences of extended joblessness.

A second measurement of cost focuses on the impact of unemployment on the federal budget in terms of both lost revenues and added expenditures. The Senate Budget Committee has estimated that for each 1 percent increase in the unemployment rate (involving an increase of about 1 million unemployed), the U.S. government lost approximately $12 billion in potential income tax revenue in 1975 and was forced to pay an additional $5 billion for such items as unemployment insurance, Medicaid, food stamps, and welfare. In addition, each 1 percent rise in joblessness was estimated to have added $6 to $7 billion to state and local budget costs through revenue losses and added expenditures. This added up to a total budgetary loss of $22 to $23 billion for each 1 percent rise in the unemployment rate.

The Congressional Budget Office has estimated that in fiscal 1977, federal program outlays for creating employment, increasing worker employability, and providing assistance to the unemployed will total $46.6 billion. This total does not include other federal, state, and local government costs that are indirectly created by unemployment, such as forgone tax revenues and increased expenditures for welfare, food stamps, and Medicaid. Nor does it take into account the added expenses of dealing with increased crime, illness, and other social problems directly correlated with higher unemployment.

Clearly, these numbers provide only a partial indication of the waste of resources caused by unemployment. Eliminating that waste goes beyond measures to secure jobs for the unemployed. The real need is to develop ways to make the most productive use of this country's total work force—of younger as well as older people, of those who could profitably work on a part-time basis, of the unskilled as well as the skilled. Among other things, this calls for eliminating job discrimination based on race, sex, or age; making productive use of persons who are now subject to mandatory retirement but who are able and eager to continue working either full or part time; giving a larger proportion of young people some work experience while they are still in school; and creating part-time or part-year jobs for parents with young children, students, older people, and others who are not able to work full time.

If the nation does not begin to utilize its available labor force more fully and productively, the burden of work will increasingly be imposed on a declining portion of the total population, thus making it more and more difficult for society to bear the growing burden of retirement costs and other social payments.

Unemployment and Inflation. High and persistent unemployment erodes the efficiency and flexibility of the economy. This further cost of unemployment stems from wasteful and inefficient use of human and physical resources as large numbers of persons who are unable to find work or to contribute to society's output have to be supported by society and as many firms are forced to operate below optimum capacity. Moreover, with general slack in the economy, the incentives for investment in both physical and human capital are reduced, and existing skills atrophy. Thus, the economy's ability to produce more during any future period of stronger demand will be handicapped, the risks of capacity and skill bottlenecks in particular areas and industries will be heightened, and inflationary price rises may be triggered more quickly.

The fear of unemployment also promotes uneconomic practices that add to costs and thus may generate further unemployment. Attempts by different groups to protect themselves against possible job losses often result in protectionist trade policies, restrictive labor-union practices, and resistance to the introduction of improved production processes. Moreover, the secondary effects of unemployment in the form of increased illness, crime, and social conflict can add significantly to living costs by raising insurance rates and causing retailers to mark up their prices.

Over shorter periods, increased cyclical unemployment can limit wage demands to some extent and enable some firms to operate more efficiently by eliminating less needed positions. Even when these factors do exert a short-term anti-inflationary influence, however, the immediate benefits must be weighed against the longer-run adverse effects of unemployment on investment, skills, and overall economic productivity.

Appropriately expansive demand-management policies (i.e., fiscal and monetary policies that affect total demand) are, of course, central to any strategy for vigorous and enduring economic growth. However, past experience has made it painfully clear that *exclusive* reliance on strongly expansive demand-management policies to stimulate growth and overcome unemployment is apt to produce high or even accelerating rates of inflation. Properly designed demand policies must be combined with a wide range of other programs in order to improve the likelihood that increased demand will lead to higher employment and output rather than to more rapidly rising prices. The main elements of such a multipronged strategy to achieve high employment without inflation will be examined in Chapter 3.

WE BELIEVE THAT CED's long-held goal of achieving noninflationary high employment must be neither modified nor abandoned. Pursuit of that goal is not only sound economics and humane social policy but also good business. *Today more than ever, there is a need for a strong national commitment to high employment that will make it possible for all those who are willing and able to work to find suitable jobs at reasonable wages within a reasonable period of time.*

Adequate job-vacancy statistics that would make it possible to measure progress toward high employment as defined in this statement are not now available. We urge that more intensive efforts be devoted to exploring the feasibility and specific means of developing adequate data in this area and that the newly appointed National Commission on Employment and Unemployment Statistics include this matter as a priority item on its agenda.

SETTING TARGETS

High employment cannot be achieved overnight. Interim targets need to be set to assure adequate progress toward the high-employment

33

goal. **Interim high-employment targets and the choice of policies for achieving them should be developed in conjunction with appropriate targets for reducing inflation.** The tasks of achieving high employment and conquering inflation are not mutually exclusive. They can and must be attacked simultaneously.

Because of the changing character and composition of the labor force and the unemployed, interim high-employment goals should not be expressed in terms of a single national unemployment rate. **We endorse the recent recommendation of the National Commission for Manpower Policy that at least three measures be used to assess the nation's progress toward high employment: the overall unemployment rate, the net change in the number of employed persons, and changes in the unemployment rates of the disadvantaged and other groups that typically experience unusually high unemployment.**

As more specific targets, we endorse the commission's suggested rate of job formation in the range of 2.5 million persons a year between now and 1980, a lowering of the overall national unemployment rate to 5 percent by the end of 1980, and a substantially more rapid reduction of unemployment rates than in past recovery periods for those segments of the labor force that tend to experience particularly difficult problems in the labor markets. We believe that these goals are both desirable and attainable *provided* they are pursued as part of a forceful and integrated overall strategy to combat both unemployment and inflation.

ELEMENTS OF THE POLICY STRATEGY

Expanding Demand. The single most effective means of reducing unemployment is a strong economy. This Committee has long been committed to appropriate demand-management policies that aim at steady but vigorous economic growth to achieve high employment. We reject prescriptions for using massive unemployment or chronic stagnation as a means of combating inflation. Such a course inhibits adequate capital formation, weakens productivity growth, and results in large-scale waste of human skills and resources. It is counterproductive over the long run.

Measures to expand effective demand must go well beyond the use of general fiscal and monetary policies to expand total spending. Within the constraints of a sound overall budget, they must also include specific sectoral policies for such purposes as revitalizing the nation's cities, rehabilitating deteriorated housing and transportation, and accelerating energy development and conservation. Many of these policies call for more effective basic approaches, rather than simply increasing government outlays. Moreover, in recessions, there is usually need for special government expenditure programs such as countercyclical public-service employment.

A vigorous and sustained demand expansion is not only needed to overcome cyclical joblessness; by and large, it is also the most effective single means of reducing structural unemployment. As labor markets tighten, the incentives for business firms to train and employ the unskilled and disadvantaged increase, the search for available workers becomes more intense, and discrimination becomes more costly. By no means all the structural problems of the more marginal labor force groups disappear as overall demand pressures increase. Nevertheless, past experience has shown that in a briskly growing economy, the scope for finding useful training and jobs for the unskilled, the poorly educated, and other structurally unemployed groups is often much greater than had previously been thought possible.

Anti-Inflation Policies. Unfortunately, the pace of demand expansion that would by itself result in a dramatic reduction in structural unemployment is also likely to create serious inflationary pressures as capacity and supply bottlenecks develop. Such a rapid expansion can also tend to produce skilled labor scarcities and serious cost-push pressures. Accordingly, demand growth should not be pushed at so rapid a pace.

To maximize the scope for demand expansion without intensified inflation, a wide range of policy measures should be used to improve the functioning of the market system, enlarge capacity and supply availability, and generally make the economy less inflation-prone. Such policies include tax and related measures to stimulate more capital investment, steps to anticipate and avert materials and skill bottlenecks, and measures to increase productivity and competitiveness.

Even if relatively vigorous demand expansion is accompanied by specific anti-inflation measures, it does not seem likely that these policies could *by themselves* reduce the overall unemployment rate to less than 5 to 5½ percent by the end of this decade without producing intensified inflation.[2] That prospect creates a major need for combining such policies

2./ The situation described here is sometimes interpreted to mean that there is no way in which unemployment can be reduced below 5 to 6 percent without a sharp

with more direct approaches for dealing with structural unemployment.

Direct Measures for Attacking Structural Unemployment. A third component of the needed policy strategy, therefore, is the use of a wide range of public and private measures specifically designed to deal with the unemployment problems of particular groups and to strengthen incentives for productive work. Such a targeted approach is needed to achieve major reductions in the chronic unemployment of groups that cannot be adequately reached by other means. Furthermore, by concentrating on high-unemployment sectors or areas in which the risks of inflation are lowest and by raising the productivity of the groups involved, it can also enable the economy to move more vigorously toward noninflationary high employment than would otherwise be possible.

Recent actions by the Administration and Congress have placed greatly increased emphasis on such measures. The new youth employment legislation, in particular, provides a major increase in targeted assistance to youth for training and work experience, and the size of the Job Corps has been doubled. Moreover, the Administration's new welfare reform proposals call for a dramatic increase in welfare clients' incentives to work and for special incentives to do so in the private sector.

The Labor Department has indicated that both the current expansion in subsidized public-service jobs and the projected additional large-scale increase in such jobs under the proposed welfare reform program are to place major focus on new types of jobs to provide needed services to local communities. These are to include improving public safety by patrolling dangerous areas and escorting people through such areas, providing home services and other aid to the elderly and the sick, building and repairing recreational facilities, expanding child-care services, assisting in weatherization of existing low-income housing and in environmental monitoring, and numerous other activities.

We welcome this increased stress on dealing more directly with structural unemployment and the announced emphasis on providing useful work. However, the precise directions that these policies are to take

---

acceleration of inflation. This is not necessarily true. As we have noted, the unemployment-inflation relationship can be changed by specific anti-inflation policies aimed at expanding capacity and supply and by measures to reduce structural unemployment. Moreover, changes in the composition of the labor force in coming years, particularly the declining proportion of teen-agers, should tend to lower the unemployment rate at which demand expansion would trigger accelerated inflation.

still need to be clarified. We believe that an effective attack on structural unemployment problems that makes optimum use of both government and private resources should be based on the following general principles:

1. Policy solutions should be carefully tailored to the character of the groups, regions, and problems involved. In particular, a clearer distinction should be made between programs designed to overcome temporary cyclical unemployment and those directed at longer-term structural problems.

2. Government policies should provide for an equitable sharing of employment and training opportunities among different target groups. Greater efforts need to be devoted to developing employment-creating strategies for individual groups, particularly teen-agers and older workers, that are complementary and mutually reinforcing rather than competitive. In cases where competition does occur, priorities should be determined in a fair and carefully considered manner.

3. The principal emphasis of public policies to deal with the unemployment problems of those who are able to work should be on providing useful job and training opportunities rather than on paying people for not working.

4. There should be a substantially greater effort to find or create these added training and job opportunities in the private sector, both profit and nonprofit. Although special public-sector training and employment programs must continue to be a substantial component of the efforts to overcome unemployment, the eventual aim of such programs is to move a high proportion of the persons covered into regular private employment. Direct placement of the unemployed in the private sector avoids the need for such a shift.

5. A range of additional incentives should be developed to help the private sector provide such opportunities, and disincentives should be eliminated.

6. Particular stress should be placed on intensified training of the disadvantaged for job vacancies that already exist.

7. There is a special need for enlarging training and employment in the small business sector. Public policies to deal with unemployment have

38

underemphasized this sector. Yet, small businesses account for about one-half of private-sector employment covered by social security[3] and play a particularly important role in many service industries, in which the potential for added employment of the young, old, and disadvantaged is especially high.

8. Public and business policies should be designed to respond to the needs and capacities of unemployed *individuals* as well as to the various groupings in which they are classified.

3./ This estimate applies if the small business sector is defined as including those firms with 100 employees or less. Firms with 500 employees or less constitute about three-fourths of private employment covered by social security.

Chapter 4
Toward a Stronger
Private-Public Partnership:
Enlarging the Private Sector's Role

WITHIN THE STRATEGY PACKAGE outlined in Chapter 3, a key feature should be the enhancement of the role of the private sector. This will require some changes in approach. The federal budget for 1977–78 provides for a substantial expansion in training and job assistance targeted to the hard-to-employ, particularly youths and the disadvantaged. However, of the total $11 billion budget program devoted to employment and training in fiscal 1978, less than 10 percent is scheduled to be devoted directly to private-sector programs. We believe that this proportion should be significantly enlarged.

THE IMPROVING CLIMATE
FOR PRIVATE-SECTOR INVOLVEMENT

Greater reliance on the private sector will not be easy to achieve. Partly because of the recent deep recession, total private-sector involvement in special training and employment programs for severely disadvantaged groups is much less today than it had been in the late 1960s and early 1970s. When private firms are forced to lay off part of their regular work force, they usually have little opportunity or inclination to provide extra training and jobs for groups that they are reluctant to employ in more normal times. But other factors also contributed to lagging private support for special training and job programs, including concern that these activities were imposing an undue burden on the firms' regular profit-making operations, disappointments with particular program results, and impatience with the red tape and lack of stability in funding and management frequently connected with federally assisted private programs.

We strongly agree that individual firms should not be asked to create training and job opportunities for special groups if this jeopardizes their efficient functioning. *But for a number of reasons, we also believe that the time is ripe for significantly increased private involvement in such activities in ways that will be sound business practice as well as good public policy.* These reasons include the following:

● If the economy is able to maintain a healthy rate of expansion, business will be in a much better position than it was in the recent period of severe recession to provide special assistance to youths, older workers, and the disadvantaged.

● Both business and government have gained valuable lessons from the experience with special training and placement efforts in the last decade and have developed a variety of new approaches that can be used to overcome past difficulties.

● There is increased recognition that the character of structural unemployment problems will be changing over the next five to ten years and that it is in the interest of business itself to search for new types of solutions to deal with these problems. Business is already finding that many skilled jobs remain unfilled. More business firms see the need for a more productive labor force, for helping to avoid further skill bottlenecks, and for providing greater flexibility in work schedules, job design, and retirement arrangements to assist youths, working parents, and older workers.

● There is increased concern that without greater private involvement, the current rapid expansion in public training and employment programs could lead to excessive increases in public-sector employment and spending and add to inflationary risks. At the same time, the feeling is growing that greater reliance on training and employment-creating activities in the private sector may in many cases prove to be more efficient and less costly.

● Both the executive branch and Congress are showing increased interest in greater private involvement in special training and employment activities. Numerous special provisions and incentives to facilitate this involvement have been included in recent legislation. In addition, the Administration's proposed welfare reform program provides strong incentives for the placement of welfare recipients in regular private-sector jobs, in part by making it financially more attractive for welfare recipients to accept such jobs rather than specially funded public-service positions.

We do not believe that any one policy prescription or type of incentive to aid the young, old, and disadvantaged will work for all firms or industries or even for different branches of a single firm operating in different parts of the country. Rather, the need is to provide business firms, labor unions, and voluntary agencies with increased *options* to make use of approaches and incentives that will help to enlarge employment and training opportunities for the groups that face special difficulties in the labor market.

PRIVATE-SECTOR APPROACHES AND INCENTIVES: INCREASING THE OPTIONS

New and Expanded Use of Private-Sector Programs that Work. Although *total* private-sector involvement dealing with employment problems has lagged in recent years, there are numerous specific instances of special training and job-creation programs conducted by private firms and nonprofit organizations that are working effectively. Many of these are new and imaginative, and quite a number represent the result of joint efforts by private firms and government manpower programs operating within the CETA framework.

These programs are often small in relation to the size of any one company's total employment, but most are of the type that could be carried out by many other companies in many more communities. *We believe that there would be a substantial increase in the private sector's contribution toward reducing structural unemployment if private programs that already work in some firms and areas were to be adopted on a wider scale nationally and by a much larger number of firms.**

*See memorandum by FRAZAR B. WILDE, page 90.

In Chapter 5, we present a number of more specific recommendations regarding key areas in which substantially wider use of existing private-sector activities could make a very substantial contribution toward solving the special employment problems of youths, older workers, and the disadvantaged. These areas include, in particular:

● Improved transition from education to work

● More productive use of older workers and retirees

● Improved job-readiness preparation, skill training, and upgrading for the disadvantaged

● Better matching of job seekers and job opportunities through greater business support for more effective public and private placement services and through development of more flexible work schedules and job arrangements

● Work sharing and other means of minimizing the volume of unemployment associated with given reductions in business activity during recessions

A major obstacle to wider use of existing private-sector programs is the fact that far too little information about the nature and results of such programs is available to the business community as a whole or to national and local government officials. The volume of case studies that we will publish on the basis of the Subcommittee's survey of CED trustee companies will cover only a part of existing private-sector activities that deserve to be more widely recognized. We believe it would be highly useful if such information could be made available on a broader and more continuous basis. **We recommend establishment of a clearinghouse for information about the character, problems, and success of private-sector programs concerned with assisting those groups in the labor force that have the highest or most persistent rates of unemployment. Such a clearinghouse might best be operated by a private organization but should receive active federal support and funding.**

Stronger Mechanisms for Active Business Participation. A key ingredient in many successful business efforts to increase training and employment opportunities has been active and coordinated support by national and local business leadership groups working closely with local community organizations, labor unions, and government units. Such nationwide organizations as the National Alliance of Businessmen can be a major element in energizing this support. However, some of the most effective cases of private participation have also involved the creation of new types of organizational mechanisms at the local level. Here are four noteworthy examples:

- In Chicago, twenty of the largest companies have combined with twenty leading minority firms and organizations to form Chicago United, which seeks to attack the city's most intractable social problems. The Chicago Alliance of Business Manpower Services (CABMS), a branch of Chicago United, is a private nonprofit organization with a permanent staff that is able to act as a direct contractor for federally financed manpower programs. This organization has been unusually innovative and effective in carrying out a wide variety of activities designed to serve the training and employment needs of marginal groups in the labor force.

- In Oak Ridge, Tennessee, Union Carbide and a group of forty-three Southern colleges and universities have been remarkably successful in jointly operating a technical training program for unskilled and disadvantaged enrollees and in assuring placement in useful jobs for over 90 percent of the program's graduates.

- With the active support of major business firms and the National Manpower Institute, a network of local education-work councils is being developed in twenty selected communities to facilitate the transition from school to work.

- The Greater Philadelphia Partnership, active since 1974, is a consortium of business leaders that fosters community development and employment in Philadelphia and particularly aids inner-city housing services and supported-work programs for the hardest-to-employ.

We urge leading business firms in communities that have not already formed such special organizations to take the initiative in developing similar cooperative ventures in a form best suited to the circumstances in their individual communites. We also urge national firms that have been leaders in successful programs in their headquarter cities to strongly encourage their local managers to help organize and support similar programs in other areas where the firms have significant operations.

This Committee has been particularly impressed by the potential of direct contracting for training and employment programs with a private nonprofit organization, such as CABMS, that is formed by a coalition of business firms. CABMS currently handles the direct marketing and management of all of the city of Chicago's federally supported on-the-job training (OJT) contracts with private and nonprofit employers. By making direct use of business experience, expertise, and innovation, this arrangement has led to a sharp reduction in the delays and red tape previously involved in awarding OJT contracts (approval time has been cut from several months to ten days), costs of training programs have been cut significantly, a large number of subcontractors (particularly smaller firms) have been brought into the OJT effort, and various innovative approaches to job placement have been developed. (See Chapter 5 for a fuller discussion.)

We recommend that government-assisted training and job programs make substantially greater use of direct contracts with private nonprofit organizations that are organized by consortia of business firms and community groups.

Strengthening Intermediate Organizations. One of the most important ways of increasing private firms' efforts to overcome structural unemployment is greater use of intermediate profit or nonprofit organizations to handle job development, training, and placement activities for groups with special problems in the labor market. For example, Opportunities Industrialization Centers of America, Inc. (OIC), a nonprofit organization founded and run by blacks that operates in forty-seven states, concentrates on skill training and job placement for members of minority groups. A recent study showed that from 1964 to 1975, 350,000 persons received OIC training, 250,000 were placed in jobs, and retention rates in these jobs were relatively high. Other examples include such community-based nonprofit groups as the Urban League; Services, Employment and Redevelopment (SER); the Boys' Clubs of America; the Vocational Foundation in New York; various organizations that aid the handicapped; and specialized agencies for the placement of older workers. Some profit-making organizations can also perform valuable intermediary functions.

It is clear that many business firms are reluctant to train or hire the disadvantaged *directly*. However, they will often do so if specialized intermediate organizations help them deal with these groups. For many firms, the use of an intermediary organization means that they can be relieved of many troublesome tasks that skill-training and other programs might ordinarily entail; this is particularly important in gaining support for such programs among line managers. Intermediate organizations can be very helpful in dealing with the red tape and complications often involved in government contracting, can concern themselves with the inevitable paper work associated with new hirings of disadvantaged workers, and can furnish needed counseling and support services to the individual trainee. Moreover, they help provide continuity for special training and related programs because they have a self-interest in seeing to it that the programs are effective and gain new funding.

Intermediary organizations can also help private firms increase the ways in which they can assist the structurally unemployed. For example, firms that are not willing to directly hire workers with special labor market disabilities can still provide physical facilities for training courses, special transportation, and technical advice. Some firms can specialize in providing technical training under contract while relying on intermediary groups to arrange for the placement of trainees. Other companies are willing to hire a specified number of persons who have graduated from special skill-training programs but prefer not to conduct these programs themselves. Specialized intermediate organizations can also be helpful in mobilizing retirees to assist in private-sector job placement of both youths and older workers. (For a fuller discussion, see Chapter 5.)

We urge that private business firms as well as government training and employment agencies give strong encouragement to greater reliance on intermediate organizations in efforts to deal with the special problems of youths, older workers, and the disadvantaged, particularly in areas of chronically high unemployment.

Greater Reliance on Jobs Corporations for Dealing with the Hard-to-Employ. In our 1970 policy statement *Training and Jobs for the Urban Poor*, we recommended the experimental introduction of a new form of intermediate nonprofit organization known as a *jobs corporation*. This corporation was designed to provide training and jobs for marginal workers and hard-core unemployed who would become the corporation's "employees" and then be placed in training and public or private employment. A special feature of the proposal was that the corporation would be partly financed by welfare and other public assistance funds that would have had to be spent on the "employees" in the absence of the program. Local management of each corporation was to be entrusted to a board of directors that included business representatives, public personnel officers, labor-union officials, and the representatives of client groups.

Since the publication of that statement, an experimental jobs corporation, the Manpower Demonstration Research Corporation (MDRC), has been established that closely follows the format suggested in the statement. MDRC is a nonprofit organization that oversees supported-work programs in thirteen different locations around the country; it currently employs about 1,900 persons. Its clients are some of the most severely disadvantaged groups in the labor force: ex-addicts, ex-offenders, long-term welfare mothers, and minority youths from low-income families. They are provided with partially subsidized (supported) work, both in the public and in the private sector, into which they are moved under conditions of "graduated stress." In time, they are expected to take on regular full-time jobs. Funding is provided primarily by government agencies and private foundations.

The results of the program (which are further discussed in Chapter 5) have been quite encouraging. An initial analysis of a sample of persons involved in the supported-work program showed that after the first nine months of the program, participants worked more hours, earned more money, and received fewer or smaller welfare payments than a control group of nonparticipants equally eligible for the program. There were additional positive results. Those in the program used drugs and alcohol less frequently and were less often involved in criminal activity.

Questions remain about whether a substantial enlargement of the present relatively small-scale experiment would encounter an equal degree of success. Nevertheless, the known experience with MDRC confirms our belief that the jobs corporation model holds special promise as an organizational mechanism for dealing with the problems of the hard-to-employ and for providing the private sector with greater opportunities to participate constructively in that effort.

One major advantage of this form of organization is that it allows strong focus on the problems of the individual. Employees can be placed in different types of training and employment on the basis of their needs and capabilities. There is a central place to which they can turn for special counseling and other assistance. At the same time, the jobs corporation can take advantage of the shifting economic situation to seek out alternative job opportunities for its clients. For example, as the economy strengthens, workers who had been placed in public employment can be shifted to suitable private job opportunities as more of these open up.

Because of the need for more aggressive efforts to deal with structural unemployment problems in the next few years, we urge a major enlargement of the existing jobs corporation effort. The possibility of

utilizing the jobs corporation format for groups other than the most severely disadvantaged should also be explored.

Legal and administrative changes to provide incentives for private-sector training and employment. As we noted earlier, recent legislation governing federal employment and training assistance contains numerous provisions that encourage wider private-sector participation. For example, part of the funds for public-service employment is to be devoted to socially useful projects that can be carried out by private nonprofit groups. The new youth employment legislation provides for a sizable amount of discretionary funds to be used for innovative programs, including those administered by the private sector. Under the newly launched program, Help through Industry Retraining and Employment (HIRE), federal subsidies are to be provided to create approximately 100,000 private-sector job-training positions over an eighteen-month period, mostly for unemployed veterans. The HIRE program is being accompanied by a new national drive to induce large corporations to take on graduates of the program as permanent employees.

Government agencies and private firms should make full use of these increased options for private-sector involvement. **We believe that the volume and scope of federally assisted on-the-job training programs should be expanded through simplification of contract procedures and extension of the HIRE program to a larger number of nonveterans.**

Another possible method of inducing employers to train or hire more of the structurally unemployed is the use of wage subsidies in the form of employment tax credits. Congress recently enacted an incremental employment tax credit that benefits firms which raise their total employment to more than 102 percent of the prior year's level. However, because the total credit is limited to $100,000 per firm, this provision is of assistance mainly to small businesses.

We have strong reservations about the economic merits of the incremental employment tax credit, mainly because of the fact that in an expanding economy, many firms will receive the credit for employees they would have hired in any case. Nevertheless, now that this tax credit has been enacted, we believe that information about its availability should be widely disseminated and that business should support efforts to conduct careful evaluations of the effects of the new approach. Moreover, the federal government should give high priority to economic and operational research regarding the use of other forms of wage subsidies as a means of creating jobs for the hard-to-employ.

Despite our reservations about the *incremental* employment tax credit, we believe that additional experimentation with *categorical* tax credits to subsidize private-sector training and employment is justified. Such credits, which apply only to specified categories of the unemployed, are more likely to add to net employment than incremental credits because they would cover groups not likely to be hired without a subsidy even after the recovery is well on its way. To be sure, there are important disadvantages in using tax credits rather than direct contracts to subsidize jobs, and we continue to favor direct contracts as the primary form of subsidy. Actual experience with one existing categorical tax credit to aid employment, the 20 percent Work Incentive Program (WIN) credit applicable to employment of welfare recipients, has been quite discouraging.

However, given the fact that direct contracts have also had only limited success in the past, we feel that further experimentation with categorical tax credits as an added tool is justified. Such tax credits might be particularly useful for small business firms, and as we have noted, expanding training and job opportunities in the small business sector deserves high priority. Moreover, we believe that improved design of a categorical tax credit may produce better results than those achieved by the WIN program. **Persons eligible for categorical credits should include not only the welfare clients now covered by the Work Incentive Program but also the long-term unemployed and lower-income groups eligible for public-service employment programs. In addition, the credits might be specifically geared to youths and older workers. Experiments might also be conducted to determine whether a higher percentage subsidy of first-year wages and decreasing subsidies in subsequent periods would prove more successful in attracting business participants.**

Reducing disincentives to private-sector training and jobs for the hard-to-employ. Existing laws and regulations contain numerous provisions that inhibit increased private employment for the young, old, and disadvantaged. Some, such as minimum wage laws and social security payroll taxes, reduce employers' demands for labor by increasing labor's price. Others, such as earning restrictions for social security and welfare recipients, hold back the supply of labor.

Before such laws and regulations are modified, however, a number of things should be determined. For example, would a change intended to aid one group cause increased unemployment for another? If so, would the change on balance still benefit the economy as a whole? Would the budget costs involved (if any) be worth the expected benefits? Could the same amount of dollars be more effectively used in a different fashion? The answers to these and related questions will vary with the type of disincentive involved and the basic demographic and economic changes.

With regard to the possible use of a differential minimum wage, for example, this Committee recommended in *Training and Jobs for the Urban Poor* that "some differentiation in [minimum wage] rates be made for the below-20 age group, the aged, and the partially disabled to avoid the real danger that employers will refuse to hire inexperienced or otherwise less productive workers at wages as high as those required for the more experienced and able." Various attempts made since that time to legislate broad-scale differentials of this type have failed. Labor unions, in particular, have been opposed to such provisions because they fear that jobs would be taken away from prime-age workers.

A number of recent studies suggest that a uniform minimum wage does have some adverse effects on the employment of teen-agers, although estimates about the extent of these effects vary considerably. There is also evidence, however, that a lower minimum wage for all teen-agers would lead to some job losses for adults. Because the main increase in new young job seekers in the next few years will come from the 20- to 24-year-old age-group rather than from the teen-age population, the question is raised whether a lower minimum wage for all teen-agers might not draw an undue number of jobs away from 20- to 24-year-olds at the very time when some of the most serious youth unemployment problems are becoming concentrated in that age-group.

For some youths, lower minimum wages already exist. The Labor Department grants about 155,000 to 175,000 exemptions from the minimum wage requirement each year to full-time students who work part time in retail and service establishments and to some other youths who participate in special training programs. The allowable quota for such exemptions is usually not filled. Procedures also exist for exempting apprentices and handicapped workers in regular private industry, but these have been used only on a very small scale. However, a sizable number of handicapped workers can be employed below the minimum wage in federally subsidized sheltered workshops, such as Goodwill Industries. Federal outlays for vocational rehabilitation of handicapped workers came to about $800 million in fiscal 1977.

We believe that before a lower minimum wage is introduced for all teen-agers, older workers, and the partially disabled, there should be additional experimentation with wider use of administrative exemptions from minimum wage requirements for selected groups and with simpli-

fied procedures for granting such exemptions.* We also believe that much more use should be made of stipends for trainees and apprentices that come to less than prevailing wages and may start below the minimum wage but are then progressively raised as the trainees gain the experience and skill needed to move into regular jobs.

Another proposed incentive to employers to hire young people would be to exempt youths under 21 from the required employer and employee contributions to social security. This would result in a payroll tax savings of about 6 percent for the employer and an equivalent increase in take-home pay for the employee. However, it would also produce a sizable loss for the social security system, which is already faced with major financing problems. Moreover, the proposed exemption would benefit many youths from relatively well-to-do backgrounds unless it was restricted to members of low-income families.[4]

More specifically targeted direct wage subsidies or categorical tax credits, such as those discussed in the preceding section, might be a more effective way to increase employer incentives for hiring teen-agers and others in greatest need of special assistance in obtaining regular employment.

In any event, we believe that careful experiments should be undertaken in selected areas to test proposals for increasing incentives for teenage employment. Because experience has shown that the long-term prospects of disadvantaged teen-agers greatly increase after they have stayed in one job for six months to a year, these experiments should also cover proposals for special incentives during the first critical year on the job. Such proposals could include exempting teen-agers from social security payments during the first year of employment or offering special bonuses and subsidies for remaining in one job for a full year.

Other possible steps involve the relaxation or elimination of the earnings limits applying to social security recipients under age 72. Under the statutory provisions in effect during 1977, a person's social security benefit was reduced by $1 for every $2 earned in excess of $250 a month ($3,000).[5] For many retirees in need of extra income, however, it would

---

4./ Restricting the exemption to low-wage *teen-agers* would not necessarily be appropriate. Recent studies show that the family income of low-wage teen-agers tends to be higher than that of high-wage teen-agers.

5./ In addition to this "implicit tax," the earnings of social security recipients are also subject to regular taxes. Consequently, the net take-home pay resulting from extra work by persons on social security could in some cases turn out to be less than the costs of working, such as transportation and lunch money.

*See memorandum by ROBERT R. NATHAN, page 90.

be far more desirable and equitable to earn the added income through productive work. To help deal with this problem, the newly enacted social security legislation provides for a rise in the social security earnings limit for persons between age 65 and age 72 to $4,000 in 1978 and for subsequent annual increases of $500 in the limit until it rises to $6,000 in 1982.

Moreover, starting in 1982, the age at which the earnings limitation no longer applies will be lowered from 72 to 70. However, the new law does not provide for total elimination of the earnings limit. Nevertheless, the issue of total elimination is likely to remain a subject of continuing congressional and public debate. Such a step, which would benefit the well-to-do as well as the needy, would entail a net cost to the social security system of perhaps $2 to $3 billion a year,[6] requiring a further increase in the combined employer-employee payroll tax if it were to be financed out of current revenues. This may not be the best way to spend several billion dollars in funds collected through the tax system, particularly in view of the fact that some of the added work performed by social security recipients could result in increased unemployment for groups in the labor force that have more urgent need for jobs.* These issues will be taken up more fully in a projected CED study of retirement reform.

These reservations do not apply to cases where added work by social security recipients could help to overcome skill bottlenecks and other labor shortages. **We reiterate the recommendation made in our 1970 statement *Further Weapons Against Inflation* that consideration be given to raising the ceiling on earnings by social security recipients in cases where such earnings are derived from work in which certified labor shortages exist.** The total current budgetary cost of such a provision would be modest. Moreover, as the economy moves closer to capacity and skill bottlenecks increase, part of or all the extra budget cost is likely to be recouped as the added availability of older workers with needed skills helps to avoid potential inflationary pressures.

6./ This cost would arise because social security benefits would have to be paid to several million persons over age 65 who work but currently cannot draw benefits because of the earnings limit. However, the net cost to the federal tax system as a whole might be less than the figure cited because social security recipients who otherwise would not have worked beyond age 65 would now become subject to income taxes.

*See memorandum by JAMES T. HILL, JR., page 91.

Chapter 5
Expanding Training and Job Opportunities for the Hardest-To-Employ: Some Key Areas for Action

IMPROVING THE TRANSITION FROM SCHOOL TO WORK

ONE OF THE MAJOR SOURCES of high youth unemployment has been the inadequate transition between education and work. For a variety of reasons, including the greater complexity of the subjects to be learned, young people today often stay in school longer than their parents and grandparents did and have little exposure to the experiences they will face when they enter regular employment. The difficulty of transition is further aggravated by the time gap that exists between the age at which young people complete their high school education (17 or 18) and the age at which employers generally begin to hire them for regular entry-level jobs. According to recent studies, about 80 percent of employers start to hire personnel for such jobs at age 21 or 22.

For many youths, neither the experience gained in school nor intermittent exposure to searching for a job and working at the kinds of jobs usually open to teen-agers is an adequate preparation for an adult career. Indeed, many are caught in a classic double bind in which they are unable

52

to get a job because they lack the right kind of work experience but cannot get the experience without a suitable job. Nor is the problem necessarily resolved once they reach the age at which firms are willing to offer them regular adult jobs. Many of these youths prove to be far less productive and adaptable than they could have been if the link between learning and earning had been stronger.[7]

An improved transition that makes school and work mutually reinforcing calls for efforts involving all segments of the community and extending through all stages of life. This is an area in which business can play an especially constructive role.

Improving Basic Education. Inadequate school preparation is proving increasingly costly for the private sector, which must often make up for these educational inadequacies through supplemental training or suffer the effects of a less productive work force. **Central to preparing workers for meaningful jobs is a significant improvement in the country's basic educational services for both youths and adults.** At a minimum, primary and secondary schools should be given clear directions and should be held accountable for seeing to it that no student is graduated who is not at least functionally literate. More generally, we consider it particularly important that expectations regarding student performance be set at a sufficiently high level and that laws for compulsory school attendance be more effectively enforced. We also believe that in designing their curricula, secondary schools as well as colleges and graduate schools need to pay closer attention to emerging changes in the types of jobs that are likely to be available.

Improving Job Information, Counseling, and Placement. One way to improve the link between school and work is to help overcome the glaring inadequacies in occupational guidance, counseling, and placement services now available to young people. In particular, there should be:

● *Better occupational information.* Young people need much more information about jobs in their communities, what these jobs are like, and what kind of preparation employers want. **We recommend**

7./ Those who enter the job market as school dropouts are often still worse off. A recently released report by the Ohio State Longitudinal Survey found that over three-fourths of high school dropouts who had aspired to additional schooling in 1966 continued to feel the need for such schooling in 1971.

that government agencies, schools, employers, and unions undertake an intensified cooperative effort to develop and distribute comprehensive occupational information. Moreover, as indicated by the current oversupply of university graduates in various professional fields, there is a major need for improved information on job prospects for college and graduate students.

● *More effective career counseling.* On average, the equivalent of the services of only about one full-time counselor for the school year is currently available for each 1,000 high school students. Moreover, much of that time is spent helping college-bound students select schools rather than helping youths who need jobs. The counselors themselves are frequently unfamiliar with the jobs and careers available. **To help overcome these gaps, we urge more active corporate and union programs that make experienced executives and other staff members available to students as career counselors on a released-time basis.** Special emphasis should be placed on retirees who can provide counseling assistance for extended periods.

● *Improved job placement assistance.* Schools and public employment services have been slow to meet the needs of students desiring work experience and high school graduates needing jobs. Improved placement services should be developed in close cooperation with employers and unions, drawing more extensively on specialized private placement agencies and involving more effective cooperation between local CETA prime sponsors and the state Employment Service offices. Business firms can also do a great deal to give students wider opportunities to visit plants and participate in special programs to acquaint them with the types of tasks these firms perform.

● *Special counseling for the most disadvantaged groups, especially minorities.* These groups have far less access to the informal job search network of employed friends and relatives that is available to other groups; their friends also tend to be severely disadvantaged in the job market. Moreover, many of these youths face special problems in relating to the most basic elements and disciplines of the adult workplace. They can benefit greatly from continuous counseling, starting early in their school career, that focuses on giving them self-confidence, teaches them how to pursue attainable goals step by step, and helps them deal with practical problems and disappointments after they obtain their initial jobs. For example, organizations such as the Boys' Clubs of America conduct regular counseling sessions for boys who start working while still in school, enabling them to share with counselors and their peers the special problems encountered in connection with their jobs.

In all these activities, there should be more stress on mobilizing the assistance of retired executives and workers on either a volunteer or a paid basis. Retirees can be of special help to youths because of their wide experience and contacts and their ability to provide special assistance for extended periods.

Integrating Classroom and Workplace. The most promising and potentially far-reaching means of bringing schools, youths, and the world of work closer together is through increasing the ways in which the teen-age years can become a time for gaining experience through *both* schooling and working. Schools need to take as part of their responsibility the arranging of work-experience opportunities and the creation of flexible classroom schedules that will allow youths to take advantage of those opportunities. Employers need to create part-time work-experience opportunities for youths still in school and to enter into joint training-education enterprises with their local school systems. Such arrangements have major direct advantages for schools, youths, and employers alike.

● Schools will be seen by youths as more relevant to the employment world, as being able to demonstrate a clearer connection between basic education and employment, and—by bringing paid work within the reach of students—as reducing the lure that employment has in attracting youths out of the schools altogether.

● Youths will have the opportunities to test the employment world *before* leaving school, to gain exposure to one or more jobs before making a choice, to work into a regular adult job on a junior apprentice basis, and to identify their educational weaknesses while there is still time to correct them.

● Employers will have the advantages of stabilizing their supply of entry-level workers through close working arrangements with the schools; of getting workers they have trained on the job and on their equipment, rather than youths with schooling but without the maturity that comes with job responsibilities; and of being able to point out to schools those educational defects in students that can be remedied by the schools before employers hire young people as regular workers.

At the high school level, at least 400,000 youths are now enrolled in some form of work or cooperative education program, and its use is expanding in postsecondary education as well.

● The Skyline Center in Dallas, Texas, is a joint effort of the schools and the business community that involves business firms intensively in career training and counseling.

● The Continental Illinois National Bank and Trust Company of Chicago has evaluated its last three years' experience with half-time employment and half-time schooling for about 500 youths and has found that work-study employees had better attendance records, retention rates, and overall performance than regular employees.

● The General Electric Company has had a long involvement with a wide variety of cooperative education programs across the country.

● A new engineering development program by Texas Instruments provides for four hours of employment each day and for four hours to attend classes at one of the participating schools in Dallas. In addition to assisting youths who would otherwise not be able to pursue an engineering degree, the program provides Texas Instruments with a source of engineering talent for the future.

Thus, integrated education and work efforts have already proved practical. They can be carried out locally. They can be started wherever a school system and employers are willing to work together. There is no need to wait for federal programs or government money (although added assistance is now available under the new youth employment legislation).

But despite the proven advantages of integrated education-work efforts, the total scope of existing programs is far less than seems feasible. For example, Chicago has a variety of well-run cooperative education programs, but they cover only 2 percent of the city's public school students. Elsewhere, some of the more promising efforts in this field have been discontinued because of recession-induced cuts in city budgets. This happened to the pioneering continuing education program in Atlanta, which operated on a four-semester basis and required high school students to have at least one-quarter of responsible work experience to be eligible for a high school diploma.

We recommend that businesses, schools, unions, nonprofit organizations, and other community groups work together to expand the volume and scope of cooperative education programs linking school and work and that the federal government make greater use of incentive funding to encourage effective work-study programs. We urge business to take the initiative in developing such cooperative arrangements.

Of course, the programs that may be developed should in no way encourage youths to leave school prematurely in order to work, nor should they downplay the inherent value of a general education.

Strengthening Vocational Education. Much more needs to be done to improve in-school vocational education. **Vocational education should be expanded and upgraded and should be brought into closer contact with the world of work and the specific needs of employers.** Moreover, some of the most successful vocational training is conducted outside the regular school systems, notably through career academies and through programs run by such groups as the Boys' Clubs of America and by 7001 (an organization that concentrates on supplementary vocational education for high school dropouts). In some cases, businesses, unions, and schools cooperate to have vocational education programs help in rehabilitating deteriorated housing in inner cities. All such efforts deserve strong encouragement and support. Serious consideration should also be given to the creation of a national extension service that would make available to workers in urban and inner-city areas the types of basic training and educational services that have long been provided for farmers through the agricultural extension service.

Other Avenues for Improving the Transition. Not all youths are best served by being in either formal education or regular jobs. For many, the important thing is merely to have work experiences that will in some way be useful to them in later life; frequently, these are the youths who have not yet made a definite career choice. Often, their main need is for exposure to the kind of work, some of it quite simple in nature, that introduces them to the elementary disciplines of a job. Others will benefit from wider opportunities for community service, particularly if such service can be usefully combined with various kinds of stipends or delayed payments in the form of tuition credits.

We welcome the fact that the recently enacted youth employment legislation substantially increases the range of such opportunities. Important additional work experience will be provided through the expansion of the Job Corps, a program that permits disadvantaged young people living in inner cities to engage in useful community work. The legislation allows other avenues for youths (primarily unemployed teen-agers from low-income families) to participate in, and obtain academic credit for, a wide range of community projects, such as neighborhood improvements, weatherization and basic repairs of low-income housing, energy conservation, and restoration of natural resources.

We also believe that job opportunities in the armed services should be taken into account in the formulation of a comprehensive policy to combat youth unemployment. Although the military experiences difficulties in attracting sufficient numbers of qualified applicants to fill the 400,000 annual vacancies, it nevertheless rejects more than 150,000 applicants a year who cannot meet physical or mental standards. We recommend closer cooperation between the new civilian programs for disadvantaged youths and the employment and training activities of the armed forces.

Job Corps centers could be used to work with rejected applicants to help them meet military entrance requirements. In addition, the Department of Labor might initiate pilot efforts to provide major assistance in securing employment or training opportunities for military personnel who leave the service before completing their first term. Such a program could help ensure that failure in the military does not result in a lifetime of failure for these youths.

Need for Community Support. An effective attack on the problem of the school-to-work transition requires strong backing and close collaboration of all the major community elements, including businesses, educators, union officials, voluntary agencies, and local CETA organizations as well as government youth service agencies. National public and private organizations can help, but the principal drive for making the programs work must come at the local level.

A number of promising initiatives have recently been instituted by private national organizations to spur the development of collaborative local efforts. The National Manpower Institute, as noted in Chapter 4, has organized a work-education consortium of twenty communities that is forming community-wide education-work councils. Similar efforts are being supported in a number of other communities by the National Alliance of Businessmen and other business and educational organizations. These programs can serve as models for greater involvement by national business firms in such community efforts.

MAKING FULLER USE OF THE OLDER WORK FORCE

Older workers (officially defined as workers over 40) often face particularly serious problems of unemployment and underemployment. If laid off in recessions, they tend to experience particularly long periods of joblessness. Many become discouraged about finding a job and drop out of the job-seeking process altogether. Even in nonrecession periods, older workers constitute a significant segment of the long-term unemployed, partly because of the lingering effects of the prior recession, partly because of skill obsolescence, partly because of age discrimination in hiring, and partly because of difficulties in finding jobs suited to their needs.

In addition, employment of older persons who want to continue working is frequently curtailed by mandatory retirement at age 65 or even earlier and by the severe limits on the total earnings permitted to social security recipients after retirement.

The personal and social losses from unemployment or wasteful use of the older work force are very serious. Many older individuals are faced with sharply rising prices, skyrocketing medical costs, and an inability to earn an adequate income through part-time or full-time work. Stress and anxieties increase as the people involved become more dependent on the financial resources of relatives and friends or on public assistance. For these people, retirement can represent an abrupt and painful shift from being able to keep up with changing economic conditions to becoming subject to events beyond their control. For society, inadequate use of older persons in the work force can represent the loss of highly valuable skills and human resources.

A major obstacle to a more productive use of older workers and retirees has been the persistence of numerous misleading stereotypes.

One such stereotype is that workers are bound to become obsolete as they move into the middle and older age-groups. Actually, a great many ways exist by which employers and government can enhance worker productivity at all stages of life. There is a major need to strengthen programs to prevent worker obsolescence while the workers are still employed, not after they have become unemployed. These programs involve effective training and retraining for adult and older workers throughout their working lives, special opportunities for developing second careers, and a variety of efforts to make more productive use of the work capabilities of retirees. Much can also be done through more flexible approaches to retirement and by creating a wider range of job opportunities specifically tailored to the needs of middle-aged and older workers.

A second widely accepted stereotype is that providing jobs for middle-aged and older workers and retirees will necessarily take jobs and income away from younger workers.* It is true, of course, that some competition for jobs among different age-groups is bound to occur. But it is by no means always true that extra work for older workers is against the interests of other age-groups.

⬤ Many jobs especially suitable for older workers, particularly retirees, do not compete with those suitable for other members of the labor force. Frequently, they involve part-time or odd-hours jobs that employers find difficult to fill. Many others call for skills or experience that younger persons do not have. Moreover, as the economy moves closer to capacity and the labor market tightens, there will be a growing need to use older workers and retirees who can provide various types of services that will be in scarce supply.

⬤ Older workers and retirees can increasingly be drawn on to perform socially needed tasks that are now being sadly neglected, including homemaker assistance to young families in which both husband and wife are working, home care to the rising number of elderly persons living alone, hospital work, and specialized counseling and job placement assistance for persons of all ages.

⬤ In many cases, extra work and income for middle-aged and older workers or retirees is of direct aid to their children and families. It often means that sons and daughters who would otherwise have to drop out of school can continue their studies and that housewives who had only started to look for work because their husbands were unemployed have the option of returning to homemaking. The ability of older persons to earn an adequate income in addition to their social security benefits can relieve their children and others in the family of major financial burdens.

● There are 30 retired social security beneficiaries for every 100 tax-payers today. If present trends remain unchanged, this ratio is expected to be 45 to 100 by 2030. Unless a larger number of older workers and retirees contribute in some way to productive work and total tax payments, the overall economic and tax burden on the rest of the population will become increasingly heavy.

A third stereotype is that the early retirement of workers during recessions is invariably less burdensome, more humane, and more effective in coping with business slowdowns than full or partial layoffs of younger workers. Again, this is not necessarily valid. (For a fuller discussion of this issue, see the final section of this chapter, "Minimizing Unemployment in Recessions.")

We urge business and government to increase training and job opportunities for midcareer and older workers as well as for retirees in ways that will make maximum use of these groups as a productive resource. This can be accomplished through a number of approaches:

Continuing Education, Skill Renewal, and Retraining. Close integration of education and the workplace should apply to workers at all stages of life, not merely to the young. Employees at all age levels should have access to continuing education and periodic opportunities for skill renewal and retraining. This applies particularly to the broad spectrum of industries and occupations where the processes of innovation and automation are producing major changes in job tasks.

Responsibility for providing such opportunities falls jointly on public and private educational institutions, employers, labor unions, and community organizations. Most communities need a substantial expansion of publicly supported adult education and training facilities.[8] As one way to assist this process, we believe that serious consideration should be given to recent proposals for using publicly supported universities to provide the same wide range of adult education and technical training facilities to urban wage earners that has long been made available to farmers through the agricultural extension service. A constructive step in this direction is the current effort by the American Association of Community

---

8./ Over the next decade, such an expansion should also help to offset the slack in demand for the services of already trained teachers and for the use of existing educational facilities that might otherwise emerge as a result of the slower growth of the school-age population.

and Junior Colleges to stimulate the provision of services by community colleges to older adults who seek work or other meaningful service. The use of government support of deferred educational grants for middle-aged and older workers should also be explored, particularly for those who have never been able to finish high school.

Even if public education facilities are expanded, much of the task of preserving and increasing the skills and interests of middle-aged and older employees must be carried out by employers, in many cases in close collaboration with unions. Many companies not only offer periodic opportunities for skill renewal and upgrading but also provide training and other assistance to employees who wish to develop a second career. Special attention should also be paid to helping women in their middle years who reenter the labor force after years as homemakers.

Reassignment and Second Careers. The extent of job changing and movement into second careers in the American economy is growing, particularly for workers over 45. More companies are finding it cost-effective to support midcareer changes by their employees through reassignment or retraining. Many firms also find it beneficial to help employees change to new careers that they can pursue elsewhere or after retirement. The mere knowledge that such options are available often makes an important contribution to employee morale and productivity, particularly in jobs involving high stress and rapid obsolescence.[9]

In view of the growing number of second careerists in their forties and fifties, business firms should reexamine their negative preconceptions about older job applicants. Apart from the fact that firms have a legal obligation not to discriminate against workers between the ages of 40 and 64, many need to take fuller account of the skills, experience, and maturity they can gain through hiring older workers.

The development of systematic career appraisal and planning systems can help detect changes in career interests, even among more experienced and skilled workers. Employees can then be assisted in reassessing career choices and making better decisions about possible changes in job assignments, work schedules, or levels of stress and responsibility.

9./ One of the most comprehensive second-career programs in the nation is conducted by the Federal Aviation Administration for its air-traffic controllers. The agency actually pays the full cost of retraining and full salary for up to two years to middle-aged air-traffic controllers who become disqualified. Although this program covers highly specialized employees in the public sector, some of its elements may be applicable to selected employment situations in the private sector.

Job Retention. Business firms should avoid unnecessary dismissals or early retirements of older and middle-aged workers because of technological changes or recessions (see "Minimizing Unemployment in Recessions"). Firms with many branches and locations can make sure that persons no longer needed in one place will have the first opportunity for openings elsewhere within the company, if necessary after some retraining financed by the firm. Johnson and Johnson, for example, has established a headquarters job bank that matches displaced or laid-off employees with specific openings in any unit of the company. Other firms that apply such practices extensively, such as IBM and General Electric, report that older workers respond with a high degree of company loyalty and a greater willingness to adapt to technological changes and reassignments.[10] Although the success recorded by these companies with such policies cannot necessarily be duplicated by firms with different products and vulnerability to cyclical patterns, elements of such policies can probably be effectively used by many more companies than is now the case.

Better Transition from Work to Retirement. Another major ingredient of policies for more productive and humane use of the older work force is to provide for a less abrupt transition from regular work to retirement and to postretirement activities. This Committee plans to deal in greater depth with issues of retirement policy in a future study. However, there are already trends that point to numerous options for improving the transition from work to retirement.

Many firms and institutions have never adopted mandatory retirement. Some have dispensed with such policies and substituted more flexible arrangements. Proposed legislation would prohibit mandatory retirement before age 70 for most workers. Exemptions are being discussed for special cases, such as college faculty members and senior corporate managers. Where mandatory age limits do apply, a great deal can be done to provide for a more gradual shift to less demanding and stressful work well before the formal retirement age is reached, including lateral transfers, shifts to permanent part-time work, and greater flexibility in work scheduling and assignments. For example, one firm permits its em-

---

10./ IBM, which since 1970 has retrained over 7,000 of its employees and relocated about 11,000, also makes it a practice to move work to facilities that have surplus people. The company reports that, as a result of its traditional policy of assuring company-wide full employment, no employee has lost any time through involuntary layoffs during the past thirty-five years, despite recessions and major product shifts.

ployees to shift to a four- or three-day workweek one year before retirement, with comparable reductions in pay. In an increasing number of cases, firms are also arranging for retirees to return to work on a part-time or nonregular basis.

Tapered retirement can help older workers and retirees to supplement their income and retain a sense of continuing usefulness through productive work. At the same time, employers are able to call on experienced and reliable personnel for a variety of special tasks. Many companies also report that a mingling of experienced older workers with younger employees leads to significant net gains in efficiency and morale.

There should also be new types of job opportunities especially tailored to the needs of older people and their employers. One such technique is the use of a *ready work force* of experienced retired personnel that is subject to recall on a part-time or full-time basis during periods of peak work loads. Another is *job sharing*, in which two persons working part time at different hours during a given day or on alternate days, weeks, or months are responsible for carrying out one full-time job.

Among noteworthy efforts by business firms and financial institutions to stimulate postretirement careers for their former employees are the following:

● Several companies in the Los Angeles area have contracted with a nonprofit agency called Second Careers to help place retirees in paying jobs, in meaningful volunteer roles, or in training to form small businesses.

● The Equitable Life Assurance Society of the United States operates its own retiree volunteer program, through which retired managers or agents are referred as consultants to community agencies that need their expertise.

● IBM provides education grants of $500 a year for five years to any older worker or retiree who wishes to develop a second career or retirement interest.

One major reason for greater use of tapered retirement and the use of retirees on a part-time or nonregular basis is the growing evidence of the adverse effects of abrupt retirement. For example, the highest suicide rates in this country are found among men aged 64 and over. Many retirees suffer from loneliness, alcoholism, or withdrawal from community and social activities. Hence, in addition to providing more part-time or nonregular work opportunities for older workers, an increasing number of employers are developing extensive preretirement and postretirement counseling assistance, often in cooperation with local unions.

We urge employers to foster a smoother transition from regular work to retirement and to valuable postretirement activities.

JOB PREPARATION, TRAINING, AND UPGRADING TO AID THE DISADVANTAGED

We believe that greatly increased private and public training opportunities should be central to any attack on persistently high unemployment, particularly for the disadvantaged.* Instead of concentrating on low-skill, dead-end jobs, the approach we favor would reduce the chronic structural unemployment problem on a permanent basis, increase productivity, and help avert potential inflationary pressures from future skill bottlenecks. Even now, many actual potential job openings exist that could be filled if properly trained personnel were available. As the economy expands more strongly, many more vacancies requiring special skills and capacities will emerge. These could be filled either by drawing directly on newly trained workers who are now unemployed or by upgrading currently employed workers and thus opening new entry-level job opportunities for the hard-to-employ.

More and better training is essential because the extraordinary longer-term changes in the economy and in the composition of available jobs are not being adequately matched by needed adaptations in the work force. The economy is becoming less dependent on muscle power and more dependent on professional, technical, and clerical skills. At the beginning of the century, over one-half of the total work force was unskilled; today, that figure is less than 10 percent. Moreover, there is a continuing shift from blue-collar to white-collar job openings, particularly in the service field. Yet, there are large numbers of people in the work force who currently lack the most elementary qualifications for filling such jobs, and existing training and education efforts for these new types of jobs are sadly inadequate.

If the disadvantaged are to help fill these needs, a wide range of special development efforts is required, aimed at job readiness, skill training, general education, counseling, job placement, and skill upgrading. As many manpower projects of the last five years have demonstrated, disadvantaged and inadequately skilled persons *can* be brought up to the performance level of other employees given time, thorough training, and special services. Many firms have found that the graduates of special programs for the disadvantaged perform as well as, or even better than, people hired through normal channels.*

Clearly, the type of preparation and training suitable for the disadvantaged and other hard-to-employ groups must vary according to the particular group involved. For young teen-agers and others with little work experience, even menial work that introduces them to the elementary disciplines of the workplace may be adequate.[11] Others need more technical or professional training. In other cases, the emphasis should be on upgrading. The following paragraphs outline key areas (in addition to improved vocational guidance and training) in which we believe that significantly stepped-up training and education efforts based on a constructive government-private partnership are particularly desirable.

There should be a major increase in the volume and coverage of apprenticeship and similar programs to enlarge the supply of highly skilled workers. Apprenticeship programs do not exist in many growth occupations in which there is a strong need for more skilled employees, especially auto repair, health care, some energy-related activities, and numerous other service jobs. Moreover, systematic training in service-sector management techniques is widely needed.

Some labor unions and some employers have been reluctant to support wider use of apprenticeship programs. **We urge government, business, and unions to cooperate in strengthening apprenticeship or comparable high-skill-training programs and in using them in a much larger number of occupations. Entry into such programs should be based solely**

11./ A corollary is that job-entry requirements for such workers should be based on their capacity for doing the jobs in question rather than on high school diplomas or purely academic tests. Although there is indeed a major need for better basic education, disadvantaged youngsters in their late teens or early twenties who have dropped out of school and are in need of jobs to support themselves should not be barred from useful work by excessive emphasis on academic credentials. A recent study by the Vocational Foundation shows that this emphasis is often a principal barrier to needed employment of the most disadvantaged inner-city youths. For many of these young people, entry into a regular job can be the alternative to "hustling" or welfare and can provide the best chance for giving them needed training and opportunities for further education.

*See memorandum by FRANCIS E. FERGUSON, page 91.

on merit, and the programs should be open to midcareer and older workers as well as to youths. We also recommend increased financial incentives for apprenticeship programs, primarily in the form of training stipends that would in some cases start below the minimum wage level and move step by step toward the going wage rate for the jobs in question. In addition, we support greater experimentation with training vouchers in connection with apprenticeship and other skill-training programs. Such vouchers could improve the quality of the training by enabling apprentices and trainees to shop around for the best available training opportunities.

Greater emphasis should be placed on expansion of on-the-job training programs. We believe that such a step-up is possible if nonprofit organizations formed by major business firms and minority enterprises can work under direct contract with CETA as turn-key operators for administering and monitoring the programs. Such an arrangement could help secure the cooperation of a significant number of smaller firms, particularly in inner-city areas. In addition, there should be wider use of training subsidies, in the form of either simplified direct contracts (mainly for larger business firms) or special incentives (mainly applicable to smaller firms). In most cases, subsidies paid should be substantially larger during the critical first six to twelve months.

More stress should be placed on private-sector training programs in poverty areas, both urban and rural. A number of such programs have been conducted successfully in the past.[12] Programs of this kind can be particularly effective in reaching unskilled youth in inner-city or rural poverty areas, where the highest unemployment rates are registered.

Federally assisted training programs should put more emphasis on upgrading employees from entry-level jobs. Appropriate career ladders are needed, supported by both on-the-job and off-the-job training and counseling. Equal employment and affirmative action programs can give a major impetus to such employee upgrading, but additional financing for CETA and related government assistance programs is also desirable.

Strong encouragement should be given to qualified private intermediate organizations that carry out job-readiness and skill-training programs in simulated work settings. These include special skill-training centers, such as those conducted by OIC, and special institutes and

---

12./ Examples are the IBM Bedford-Stuyvesant facility in Brooklyn, Control Data Corporation plants in Minneapolis and in Washington, D.C., and a computer plant in Kentucky using a rural poverty work force.

training centers sponsored by individual corporations. Much wider use should be made of highly focused technical training programs, such as the Training and Technology program in Oak Ridge, Tennessee (cited in Chapter 4). In that joint effort by government, universities, and private corporations, training is closely linked to the employers' needs and to the job market in technical occupations. In this instance, the trainees—most of whom are young and disadvantaged—are trained in a factory setting, according to actual plant rules and discipline, by instructors furnished by Union Carbide.

There should be increased efforts to draw gifted minority individuals and women into professional fields where they have been largely absent, such as engineering, the higher levels of business administration, accounting, law, and medicine. These people need various kinds of special training and support, often at younger ages. One excellent example is provided by INROADS, Inc., an organization incorporated in five cities (Chicago, Saint Louis, Milwaukee, Cleveland, and Pittsburgh) that is supported by government funds and by major corporations. INROADS provides precollege and college training for the gifted poor from black and Hispanic backgrounds to help prepare them for business and engineering careers. With the help of corporations and educational institutions, a considerable number of other organizations have also been established to increase the proportion of minorities entering engineering. With added organizational efforts and incentives, the number and scope of such programs could be substantially increased.

Very special kinds of training must be offered to the most severely disadvantaged who have basic difficulties in relating to the world of work. This type of training, often in the form of supported work, involves learning job discipline, punctuality, relationships to supervisors and peers, and a sense of quality control. As indicated in Chapter 4, we believe that for this group, a major expansion in the use of jobs corporations is appropriate.

BETTER MATCHING
OF JOB SEEKERS AND JOBS

Increased employment for youths, older workers, and the disadvantaged depends on better education and training as well as on breaking down legal barriers to their employment, inflexible industry and union practices, and discrimination. But even when persons in the target groups have become job-ready and when vacancies exist, there are often major problems in matching these job seekers with suitable job opportunities. This section focuses on a number of approaches for helping to deal with this problem that we regard as particularly promising and that call for greater private initiatives or public-private cooperation.

Strengthening the Employment Service. The United States Employment Service (ES) has special responsibilities and opportunities to find jobs for groups with particular difficulties in labor markets. Yet, its overall contribution toward this goal has fallen far short of what seems either possible or desirable. We believe there is need for a far more aggressive effort than has yet been mounted to make the Service more effective. In Chapter 6, we discuss ways in which the Employment Service can be improved through organizational changes, notably much closer coordination with federally assisted CETA programs. Various other improvements, such as expansion of computerized job banks to include listings of both job applicants and job openings, are also urgently needed.

A central requirement for increased effectiveness of the Employment Service is establishment of a more productive relationship with employers. The Service has little chance of success if employers will not list their job openings with it. This aspect of the Service's operations has often been badly neglected, but in the last few years, ES has made a special effort to improve its services to employers. Although some of these efforts have been encouraging, they have been carried out in only about 10 percent of the local ES offices. **We urge that a much more forceful effort be made to develop improved services to employers by Employment Service offices throughout the country.**

One of the best ways to cement a mutually beneficial relationship between the Employment Service and employers is the use of Account Representatives. Under this arrangement (which has been used with particular success in Chicago and Pittsburgh), potential employers deal with a single designated ES officer, a process that provides accountability and continuity of service. Each ES Account Representative is assigned a block of companies, preferably those with similar occupational lines, and assumes full responsibility for all job orders, including screening, referral, verification, and other follow-up functions.

This procedure permits the Account Representative to work closely with selected companies and to develop expertise in filling their needs. **We urge further development and wider use of the Account Representa-**

tive system. We also recommend further development of the practice, already followed in some centers, that involves personnel exchanges between the ES offices and given employers in the interest of a better reciprocal understanding of needs and services.

The Account Representative system should be combined with increased use of applicant officers in CETA prime sponsor offices. These officers would be responsible for a block of applicants and would follow each applicant from admission to the program through training and referral for placement. Particular applicant officers should specialize in handling older people, younger persons, or the disadvantaged. In effect, these applicant officers would become ombudsmen for persons with special difficulties in entering the labor market; they would advise Account Representatives about the best strategy for placing such persons. The applicant-officer function can also be subcontracted to private employment agencies that have special interest and expertise in the problems of particular groups, such as older workers. (See "A Larger Role for Specialized Job-Finding Agencies.")

We believe that this arrangement will be more effective in placing special client groups than the existing formal requirements for assigning priorities to certain groups. By working closely with both employers and CETA, Account Representatives may also be able to negotiate agreements to hire more of the disadvantaged, old, or young. In this way, they not only fill an employer's job needs but also help employers to fulfill their affirmative action obligations.

A Larger Role for Specialized Private Job-finding Agencies. For many of the hardest-to-employ, in good times as well as in recessions, the usual kind of job placement efforts carried out by the Employment Service and regular employment agencies are simply not enough. These people include our most severely disadvantaged youths, many of whom are school dropouts or have criminal records or drug problems or are handicapped, and many older persons who may be entirely job-ready but who have become discouraged from searching for a job because of the difficulties of locating suitable opportunities on their own.

For these groups, it is not enough to point out job openings listed by employers. Instead, an intensive effort is required to seek out or develop job opportunities that fit their individual capabilities and requirements. In many cases, it calls for special full-time or part-time jobs for which somebody is willing to pay but which are currently nonexistent. Often, it also calls for seeking out disadvantaged persons for whom job openings are available but who are unaware that such opportunities exist. In fact, it is quite common for agencies specializing in this work to succeed in developing more job opportunities for disadvantaged workers than they are able to fill from their current pool of job seekers.

Such tasks can in part be carried out through the vocational training and guidance work of secondary schools, by CETA and other public agencies, and by community-based organizations that also carry out other functions. But we believe that there is particular promise in wider use of specialized nonprofit job placement agencies for the difficult-to-employ that receive partial support from public funds. A number of such organizations already exist and have had notable success in particular communities.

● The Vocational Foundation in New York City, which has operated since 1936, finds jobs for disadvantaged youngsters 16 to 19 years of age who have had some past trouble with delinquency and have few marketable skills. In 1976, the foundation dealt with 2,400 youths, developed 3,700 job openings, and placed about 1,100 youths in jobs. (Before the recent recession and New York's financial crisis, the total number of placements was about 3,000 a year.) Although this organization has had a remarkable record as an employment agency of last resort, its specialized services reach only a small proportion of the total number of youths in New York City who need this kind of assistance. Furthermore, in most cities, this type of service is simply not available.

● Various intermediary nonprofit organizations in many communities bring together employers and older workers. Two of the largest of these are Retirement Jobs Inc., in the San Francisco area, and the Senior Personnel Employment Committee in White Plains, New York. Both operate a number of offices in their target areas and use both volunteer and paid older workers for job development and referral functions. The Senior Personnel Employment Committee, which has existed for about twenty-five years, currently finds jobs for about 700 older workers annually.

These specialized agencies provide highly individualized counseling and support services both before and after placement or training. The Vocational Foundation has found that such services make a critical difference in job-retention rates for the youths they place. Without such support, half of these youths usually drop out of the work force in the crucial first six weeks.

Another important advantage of specialized private agencies is their ability to develop suitable job opportunities with medium-sized and smaller firms. Many of the jobs suitable for the hardest-to-employ are with small firms, particularly in the service industries. Yet, these very firms often do not use regular private employment agencies or the Employment Service. However, once contacted by a representative of a specialized job-finding agency, smaller firms are often more receptive than larger ones to hiring youths as well as older workers because their recruitment specifications tend to be less formal. Moreover, both young and older persons who have had difficulty in securing jobs often respond more favorably to the more informal atmosphere of smaller firms.

Although such agencies perform useful services, they reach only a small proportion of the people who need assistance. **We urge that government and the private sector support wider use of specialized private job placement agencies for hard-to-employ groups.** Such an effort should include these major ingredients:

● Business leaders, working with government and community groups and federal manpower programs, should take the initiative in encouraging the creation of such agencies in areas where they do not now exist. Very often, all that is involved is the addition of this function to programs of existing agencies.

● Government agencies, including the Employment Service and CETA, should subcontract with specialized private job-finding agencies to help cope with the special placement needs of disadvantaged persons.

● Financial incentives should be used much more aggressively to encourage creative entrepreneurship in the placement of hard-to-employ youths. We urge federal support, through CETA or other suitable agencies, for responsible private job-finding agencies that pay commissions to job developers working full or part time. The amount of commissions payable under such government contracts should be liberal enough to provide strong incentives for a major increase in the volume and intensity of job-finding activities. Commissions would have to be contingent on verification of placement and a minimum period of job retention. Moreover, the private job-finding agencies aided by public funds should be held accountable for high-quality service provided by its commission workers.

● In staffing these agencies, major emphasis should be placed on the use of qualified older persons, both as commission workers and as volunteers. This practice is already successfully used by many existing agencies. **As a special incentive for increased reliance on older persons, we urge that commissions or other remuneration paid to job developers in qualified job-finding agencies be exempt from the limitation on earnings applicable to social security recipients.**

This approach would help solve two persistent unemployment problems simultaneously. It would provide many older persons with part- or full-time work and at the same time bring to the young the experience, know-how, and network of contacts of people who have the time and patience to find ways of remedying the deficiencies and removing the obstacles that have made employment for young people so difficult.

Many older persons are already known to be efficient job developers, in part because of their wide familiarity with employers.[13] With a special stress on older staffers and greater financial incentives, it should be feasible to enlist a much larger number of qualified job developers than is now possible.

Adapting Jobs to People: Alternative Work Patterns and Designs. Often, a better match between people and jobs will call for basic changes in the nature of the jobs themselves. Most jobs are still designed for prime-age, full-time workers operating in a factory, office, or store on a relatively rigid time schedule. However, because of changes in the composition of the labor force and in life-styles, there are many people today who are willing and eager to work but who find that they do not or cannot fit into such a restricted job design. For these people, getting jobs and becoming productive members of the labor force often depend upon the availability of work opportunities more closely tailored to their needs, such as flexible hours and part-time work.

Such people include youths who are still in school or are participating in special training programs, working parents with children and other home responsibilities, older workers who need relief from high-stress work

---

13./ According to a 1974 Louis Harris survey, 135,000 Americans who are 65 or older are already engaged as volunteers in providing employment services.

schedules, and retirees who are only able to work part time and are subject to social security limitations on outside earnings. Such alternative work arrangements are especially important for the disadvantaged, such as women heads of households on welfare who want to work but must devote part of their time to taking care of school-age children. But alternative kinds of work opportunities are often also needed to attract a larger proportion of high-skilled workers into the labor force and thereby reduce the risks of future skill bottlenecks.

Flexible working hours are now being used in over 6,000 European companies and have been adopted by several hundred larger American concerns. "Flextime" is now being given a three-year test in certain federal agencies. Some of the larger private firms that have used this technique, such as the Metropolitan Life Insurance Company in New York, have found that it increases employee morale and sense of responsibility, reduces absenteeism, and improves productivity.

Part-time employees are one of the fastest-growing components of the U.S. work force. As recently as 1970, 1 out of every 8 workers was a part-timer. Today, 1 out of every 5½ employees works part time. About two-thirds of all part-time employees are adult women. Reliance on part-time work is widespread among teen-agers and persons over 60.

Although many part-time jobs are temporary and involve only short hours, a growing number of part-timers work on a permanent schedule. Permanent part-timers, many of whom are older housewives with fixed family responsibilities, are used on a large scale by department stores and other retail outlets, insurance companies, and financial institutions. Many manufacturers are also making substantial use of part-time workers. For example, one large pharmaceutical company has a part-time work force that is three times as large as its full-time work contingent. These employers find that part-timers do not fit the stereotype of marginal, temporary, or uncommitted workers. They are a stable work force of individuals who want regular but not full-time work.

Business firms are increasing their use of special work schedules that fit the requirements of particular groups of workers as well as the requirements of the firm. For example, in some companies, older workers are employed on a schedule of two or three days a week as well as on special shifts. Other special time arrangements that can be particularly helpful to older workers include job sharing and job alternating and the use of a ready work force of retirees subject to call during peak load periods. Another promising arrangement enables parents to work only during those months when their children are in school.

Significant increases in work opportunities can also result from changes in the design and location of jobs. As we have noted, some firms make active efforts to taper down the work responsibilities of employees as they approach retirement age. Conversely, various techniques can be used to gradually increase the demands on workers in supported-work programs. In the future, technological changes may make it practicable for an increasing number of tasks now performed in factories and offices to be carried out at home. This could apply, for example, to many types of complex technical calculations that can be performed with the aid of a computer terminal.

In our view, a broadening of options for the use of alternative work patterns could make a significant contribution toward reducing the more intractable forms of unemployment and underemployment. At the same time, such options can do much to contribute to greater business efficiency and flexibility in operations. **We recommend that employers review the organization and scheduling of their work flow to determine whether more job opportunities could be created for youths, the disadvantaged, older workers, and retirees through development of a wider range of alternative work patterns, including more part-time work and nonregular employment.**

MINIMIZING
UNEMPLOYMENT IN RECESSIONS

Although recessions usually stem from widespread reductions in overall demand and output, their adverse effects on jobs and earnings tend to fall disproportionately on those members of the work force who lose their jobs or who are unable to secure new jobs. For many of these people, unemployment is compounded by the loss of medical and other social benefits, reduced self-confidence, increased personal stress, and erosion of skills.

The groups that suffer most in recessions are frequently the same ones that are particularly vulnerable at other times. Youths and the disadvantaged are often among the first to be laid off. Older workers are more protected through seniority rules, but once laid off, they face greater difficulties in finding new jobs. They are also often pressured to opt for early retirement, even when that is not in their own best interest.

Clearly, the principal response to recessions should be a set of fiscal and monetary policies that will restore adequate levels of total demand

and output. Because it takes time before such policies can become fully effective, antirecession measures should also include adequate provisions to cushion the impact on individuals through unemployment compensation and other income-maintenance payments, plus steps to provide new temporary job opportunities through public employment. Recent antirecession strategies have made active use of all these approaches.

We believe, however, that there is need for a harder look at an additional approach: namely, more systematic efforts to minimize outright layoffs and forced idleness during recessions.

First, business firms should, wherever feasible, fully explore alternatives to outright layoffs when their sales volume is reduced as a result of recessions. The scope of such alternatives will, of course, vary greatly for different companies and in different situations. Firms should not be asked to retain employees where this runs counter to the companies' longer-term productivity. However, we believe that a careful assessment of longer-term costs and benefits would uncover a larger number of instances in which the companies would benefit from a reduced number of dismissals.

Without a careful cost-benefit analysis, companies may underestimate the extent to which outright layoffs in recessions are now often more costly or represent less of a saving than in the past, especially where increased training costs have substantially added to the capital value of current employees and where the cost of searching for qualified new employees is high. Conflicts between seniority and equal employment rights have also increased the costs of layoffs, resulting in extra legal expenses as well as morale problems. At the same time, the savings from layoffs have often been reduced because of increased company contributions to unemployment compensation and supplementary benefit payments.

Second, the federal government should actively encourage corporate policies to provide skill-upgrading programs and other training opportunities as alternatives to layoffs in recessions. There should be standby authorization for enlarged government subsidies for such programs that could be automatically made available when national and area unemployment rises above specified levels. These subsidies should be available not only to companies that provide on-the-job training for their own employees but also to firms that initiate special training programs for unemployed persons who will subsequently be placed with other employers. The net cost to the government of supporting such training and education programs during recessions will be relatively low because the beneficiaries of these programs would have received unemployment insurance or some other form of government support in any case.[14]

Third, we recommend active exploration of possible legal and administrative changes to facilitate work sharing as an alternative to cyclical layoffs in cases where such a solution is desired by both management and labor. Work sharing can be important in reducing the uneven burdens that now fall on a limited number of employees with the least seniority during recessions. Furthermore, because work sharing avoids layoffs altogether, it can be particularly useful in preventing conflicts between seniority and equal employment considerations during recessions.

The needed administrative or statutory changes might include allowing payment of unemployment insurance for single days in cases in which work schedules have been cut to four days (although this arrangement might have to be limited to companies that have bona fide work-sharing programs and are located in areas of high unemployment), permitting workers in plants operating at reduced capacity to work on alternate weeks and draw unemployment insurance when not working (along lines that have already been successfully tried in the state of Connecticut), and compensatory payments to employers for increased per unit cost of medical and other fringe benefits that result from work-sharing arrangements. It should be emphasized that our recommendations relate to work sharing only as an alternative to cyclical layoffs; consideration of the issues involved in wider use of work sharing and shorter hours over the longer term is beyond the scope of this statement. Moreover, our comments concern the kind of work sharing that produces four days' work for four days' pay, not four days' work for five days' pay.

Fourth, substantially greater efforts should be made to assure that persons now receiving unemployment insurance payments during recessions be given more active opportunities and encouragement to benefit from useful training or work opportunities. More specifically, we recommend that recipients of unemployment insurance be able to participate in retraining and education programs within a reasonable period after they receive their initial unemployment insurance checks. Participation in such

---

14./ In the case of programs of this type run during the last recession by General Electric and by Zenith Radio, net costs to the government came to only about one-third of the cost of normal government-funded training activities.

programs (where available) is now required for persons who have drawn unemployment insurance benefits for more than thirty-nine weeks. We believe that, where feasible, such a requirement should be made effective considerably sooner (after twenty-six weeks or even earlier). Moreover, in future recessions, greater efforts should be made wherever possible to find better alternatives to such extended eligibility periods for unemployment benefits as the sixty-five-week maximum period used in the last recession. In particular, more advance arrangements should be made to provide training and subsidized public or private work opportunities to the unemployed after their unemployment insurance has expired.

In applying any of these prescriptions, great care will have to be taken to assure that there is no undue interference with layoffs and job search efforts needed to allow permanent resettlement of workers whose jobs have become outmoded or who are operating in distressed firms, industries, or localities. For such workers, more relocation and retraining assistance will often be desirable.

Chapter 6
More Effective Management
of Federally Assisted Employment
and Training Programs

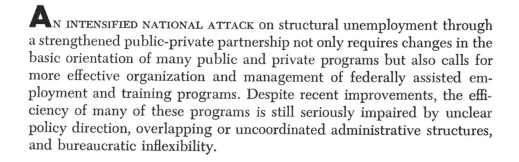

AN INTENSIFIED NATIONAL ATTACK on structural unemployment through a strengthened public-private partnership not only requires changes in the basic orientation of many public and private programs but also calls for more effective organization and management of federally assisted employment and training programs. Despite recent improvements, the efficiency of many of these programs is still seriously impaired by unclear policy direction, overlapping or uncoordinated administrative structures, and bureaucratic inflexibility.

THE CURRENT ADMINISTRATIVE STRUCTURE

Since CED called for a range of reforms in the administration of federally assisted employment and training programs in *Training and Jobs for the Urban Poor*, a number of far-reaching changes in the administration of federal manpower programs have been instituted. Most important among these were the enactment of the Comprehensive Employment and Training Act (CETA) in 1973, the creation of a temporary countercyclical public-service employment (PSE) program in 1971 and the revival of such a program in 1974, recent improvements in the legislation governing that program, and the enactment of the 1977 Youth Employment Act.

As its title implies, CETA was designed to substitute a comprehensive and integrated approach to federally assisted employment and training programs for the more than twenty existing categorical manpower programs that had been administered by a wide range of separate and often competing bureaucracies. CETA's main features are decentralization and decategorization. Primary responsibility for planning and delivery of manpower services was shifted from the federal government to state and local government units, although these remain subject to federal oversight. It was hoped that this change would make it possible to gear these services more closely to the unique characteristics of local labor markets. The basic focus of the overall program continued to be on preparing the hard-to-employ for self-sustaining jobs. However, in place of the many federal directives regarding categories of unemployed to be served, decisions about priorities were to be made primarily at the local level.

Some 445 prime sponsors (mostly state and local governments) have been organized under the act. These prime sponsors engage in training and placement programs, principally through subcontracts with various public agencies and public or nonprofit community-based organizations, including those that serve racial and ethnic minorities or other specialized clienteles.

In an important number of instances, this arrangement has resulted in more comprehensive and innovative approaches to the delivery of manpower services at local and regional levels. But there have also been many areas where performance under the program has been far from satisfactory. The following are some of the principal difficulties that have been encountered:

● Although CETA was created primarily to help the structurally unemployed, the severe recession of 1974–75 resulted in a widespread reallocation of CETA funds toward support of countercyclical public-service employment. Thus, CETA funds originally intended for disadvantaged groups were often used to avert layoffs of regular city workers, particularly policemen, firemen, and other essential employees. As a result, a high proportion of CETA clients has turned out to consist of middle-income whites rather than members of minority groups or others who encounter chronic difficulty in obtaining employment.

● The rearrangement of functions among federal, state, and local officials has in many cases proved to be less than ideal. Under the previous system, federal control over local activities may often have been too tight and too narrowly pinpointed to particular categories of the unemployed. The pendulum now frequently appears to have swung too far in the other direction.

● The fact that the U.S. Employment Service continues to be run as a separate manpower system under state control continues to fragment federally assisted manpower services. At the local level, rivalry between the Employment Service and CETA often remains intense, resulting in considerable inefficiency and duplication of effort. For example, in many jurisdictions, the local ES offices do not share job-bank information with CETA prime sponsors.

KEY REQUIREMENTS
FOR IMPROVING THE SYSTEM

It is still too early for a full evaluation of the experience under CETA, particularly because the special difficulties that have arisen as a result of the recession are diminishing in importance and because recent basic changes in the CETA legislation should help channel a higher proportion of CETA funds to the disadvantaged and the long-term unemployed. Nevertheless, we believe that there is need for a major effort to strengthen and revitalize the structure and administration of federally assisted employment and training services. An effective system for planning and delivery of these services should

● be subject to clear and integrated direction at all levels of government

● place principal responsibility for delivery of services at the regional and local community levels but provide for sufficient federal direction to assure that appropriate local coordination is in fact caried out

● provide strong incentives for increased involvement of the private sector (profit as well as nonprofit) in the development and implementation of training and employment programs

• clearly distinguish between broad categories of employment programs that are designed to serve different types of needs: the elimination of cyclical unemployment, the enlargement of training and employment opportunities for groups that experience special difficulties in the labor market but are basically able to cope with work, and assistance to the most severely disadvantaged groups that are not able to cope with the world of work without major additional aid

The administrative improvements described in the remainder of this chapter would be especially helpful in fostering a stronger public-private partnership.

REALIGNING FEDERAL, STATE, REGIONAL, AND LOCAL FUNCTIONS

To eliminate the existing duplication of U.S. Employment Service and CETA functions, we recommend that appropriate administrative and, if necessary, legislative actions be taken to bring the two organizations into a closely integrated structure from the Department of Labor down through regional, state, local, and neighborhood offices.* This will require strong directives to produce both the needed integration at each level of government and adequate flexibility to allow for diverse needs and circumstances in different states and local areas.

Our stress on stronger federal oversight does not mean that the trend toward shifting responsibility for integrated delivery of manpower services to regional and local levels should be reversed. On the contrary, we believe that, subject to federal standards and performance audits, regions and local communities should be given increasing responsibility for carrying out these functions. But this increased delegation of operational functions to regional and local jurisdictions that receive federal assistance should not give such jurisdictions discretion to adopt a do-nothing approach or to tolerate continued wasteful duplication of services. Nor should it allow such jurisdictions to ignore the need for greater and more imaginative efforts to involve the business sector, labor unions, private nonprofit organizations, schools, and other elements of the local community more fully in CETA activities along the lines recommended in Chapter 4.

The federal government needs to give more forceful and explicit encouragement to CETA programs that foster active community participation and to an enlarged role for the private sector. It can do this in part by technical assistance and incentive funding for community programs that move in this direction and by more systematic efforts to provide information about successful instances of public-private cooperation to government units and private firms throughout the country. In this connection, we recommend that the Secretary of Labor be authorized to allocate up to 20 percent of CETA funds at his discretion to prime sponsors whose performance merits special recognition and support. (Such an allocation would be in addition to discretionary funds already available for other purposes.)

The regional offices of the Employment and Training Administration (ETA) should be a focal point for encouraging greater local community participation in the design and administration of manpower programs. Regional ETA offices should, at a minimum, develop explicit cooperative arrangements between the Employment Service and CETA. Where possible, however, they should aim at developing arrangements that will allow unified local agencies to become the operating arms of both the federal and the state governments in providing a full spectrum of employment and training programs.

This process should be started now. In some states and for selected prime sponsors who have demonstrated strong administrative competence, state governors could negotiate the assumption of Employment Service functions by local authorities under subcontracting arrangements. Moreover, in local areas or neighborhoods where structural unemployment is particularly acute—and eventually, in other areas as well—regional ETA administrators should take the initiative in establishing comprehensive manpower service centers. Such centers would bring under integrated administration the full range of federally assisted manpower services, including those provided by ES and CETA. Where possible, private-sector agencies providing manpower services to structurally disadvantaged groups should also be included in these centers.

CLARIFYING EMPLOYMENT SERVICE AND CETA FUNCTIONS

The Employment Service should be clearly recognized as having the main responsibility among public agencies for *labor-exchange* functions, including job referral and placement of the best-qualified candidates for available employment opportunities. The role of CETA should be devoted primarily to *employability development* of the disadvantaged and other groups that encounter special difficulties in participating in the labor market. Under this arrangement, the Service should normally screen applicants, refer those who are not job-ready to CETA prime sponsors for training and supplementary services, and be staffed and organized to offer placement services to CETA participants who are job-ready.

The Labor Department should make the separate functions of the Employment Service and CETA clear. We recommend, moreover, that ETA regional administrators be authorized to require each prime sponsor and related state Employment Service office to agree on their respective functions and on means of cooperation, subject to the approval and subsequent monitoring by the regional administrator.

Putting most referral control in ES offices does not mean that CETA organizations and their contractors would or should be prohibited from all job development and placement activities. Many of these organizations have unique capacities for opening job opportunities to their clients who have completed periods of special training. Provided they are adequately coordinated with ES, CETA placement efforts on behalf of the disadvantaged as well as young and older workers will remain highly useful.

FURTHER WAYS TO MAKE
THE EMPLOYMENT SERVICE MORE EFFECTIVE

In addition to this clarification of ES functions and the use of Account Representatives and other reforms discussed in Chapter 5, the effectiveness of the Employment Service can be increased by relieving the Service of unnecessary requirements and functions.

The Employment Service has long been faced with a basic dilemma: On the one hand, its effectiveness depends on inducing employers to list suitable job vacancies with it. This, in turn, is likely to occur only if employers know that the Service will present the best available candidates for placement in response to job orders. On the other hand, ES is under legal and other mandates to give preference in job referrals to a wide array of priority categories of people, thus reducing its ability to offer the best candidates. The number of these mandated priority categories has become so large that the whole preferential system has become counterproductive.

We are convinced that more job opportunities will open up for the disadvantaged as well as the other hard-to-employ groups under a system that attracts a broader mix of employer job orders than those that can be filled by applicants of marginal employability. **We recommend that except for veterans who must be accorded preference by statute and migrant and seasonal workers under judicial mandate, the present list of placement priorities stipulated by administrative regulation should be abandoned.** Instead, provisions should be made to assure that sufficient consideration is given to the long-term unemployed, those claiming unemployment insurance benefits after fifteen weeks of unemployment, and registrants under aid for dependent children.

Of course, the Employment Service must adhere strictly to the requirements of equal employment opportunity laws. Furthermore, the changed policy should not relieve the Service of its obligation to cooperate with CETA in the placement of the hard-core unemployed. However, such referrals should meet basic qualification standards.

The ability of the Employment Service to carry out its basic labor-exchange functions is currently also seriously impeded by its legal obligation to carry out a wide variety of enforcement and compliance responsibilities not directly related to its basic mission. It is required to inspect business premises for compliance with safety and health regulations, the Civil Rights Act, and numerous other statutes. This not only preempts an undue share of ES resources but also increases employer reluctance to rely on the Service for job referrals. With the emergence of new regulatory agencies in specific fields related to the workplace (e.g., the Occupational Safety and Health Administration, the Office of Federal Contract Compliance, and the Equal Employment Opportunity Commission), numerous ES enforcement and compliance activities have become redundant.

In the interest of upgrading Employment Service labor-exchange functions, we urge that a systematic review be undertaken to determine what enforcement responsibilities are not essential to those functions and can be transferred to other federal or state agencies without in any way weakening antidiscrimination and other protective social legislation.

COUNTERCYCLICAL AND STRUCTURAL MANPOWER PROGRAMS

As we indicated earlier, many of the recent difficulties in implementing employment and training programs aimed at the hard-to-employ and at securing greater private-sector involvement in this connection stemmed from the fact that during the recession, countercyclical public-service employment often tended to crowd out such programs.

There is a clear need for both types of measures. Although they overlap to some extent, they tend to be directed at different segments of the population, to involve different time horizons, and to call for distinctive policy approaches and administrative structures.

To be most effective, programs to train and place the structurally unemployed should be clearly separated from countercyclical unemployment measures in terms of both allocation and administration at the state and local levels, although all such manpower services should be concentrated under the direction of the Department of Labor. Specifically, funds provided under Title VI of CETA (which covers countercyclical public-service employment assistance) should not be unduly mixed with or substituted for funds intended for the long-term structurally unemployed and for reducing unemployment in distressed areas (Title I and Title II).

To meet these requirements, the legislation governing countercyclical public-service employment was recently changed to assure that more PSE jobs go to those most in need and that they are not simply used to support ongoing government services. Thus, the law now requires that a substantial and rising proportion of CETA enrollees meet an income test and that they must have been unemployed for fifteen weeks or more, exhausted their unemployment benefits, or be on welfare. Also, to minimize substitution, most CETA public-service employment jobs must now be for specific projects of no more than one year's duration. In addition, the project emphasis should permit significantly greater involvement of nonprofit and community-based organizations. These changes in the law are laudable and should result in making PSE programs both more effective and more directly responsive to needs.

However, we believe that additional changes are needed to make PSE more countercyclical and to avoid carrying enrollees in PSE jobs for periods of several years. **We recommend that no individual be retained in a public-service employment job for more than a year (or perhaps a longer specified period at times when the national unemployment rate exceeds a specified figure).** This limitation would give many more difficult-to-place participants an opportunity to gain valuable work experience and yet give them an incentive to continue their search for regular employment.

Many of the recent problems with employment and training programs emerged because adequate countercyclical programs were not in effect when the recession hit. To reduce such problems in the future and to increase the likelihood that needed steps will be taken on a systematic rather than on an ad hoc basis, we urge that more advance thought and preparation be devoted to the types and contents of measures that might be called for and to procedures that would allow appropriate antirecessionary actions to be taken in a timely fashion and without adverse effects on existing programs to cope with long-term structural unemployment.

Taken together with the other measures recommended in this statement, we believe that the changes in the organization and administration of federally aided employment and training programs proposed here would do much to improve the job prospects of hard-to-employ Americans.

Memoranda of Comment, Reservation, or Dissent

Page 12, by R. STEWART RAUCH, JR.

This statement is not valid under all circumstances, and it is not a helpful guide to policy at the present time. Adequate demand is a *sine qua non* for high employment, but the chief concern now is that many structural barriers interfere with the job placement of the hard-to-employ. Such barriers have not been destroyed by past periods of high demand for goods and services. In fact, the speed and nature of technological change and geographic shifts have made many structural barriers more resistant to generalized demand pressures.

Page 13, by HENRY B. SCHACHT

This statement effectively deals with structural unemployment on the assumption that there is an additional need for labor in the private sector if it can be better trained and identified. Given this assumption, the private-sector experimentation on job-related issues is gratifying; government programs should be better organized to create additional incentives for these programs. It is beyond the scope of this statement to analyze whether, given inflationary pressures and prospective slower economic growth, private-sector demand can sustain full employment. If job demand should prove inadequate, then greater consideration should be given to public jobs programs and/or other forms of public assistance.

Page 15, by JAMES Q. RIORDAN

I disapprove of the statement.

I do not think that a solution to the problems of employment can be achieved with additional detailed initiatives developed in the public sector. In a public-private partnership, the public (i.e., the government) is inevitably the senior partner. In our democratic society, the senior partner's decisions must reflect political compromises. Political compromises result in inconsistent push-pull directives. The resulting administration is often costly and confused.

We should not be surprised in these circumstances to find that an elderly citizen is "encouraged" to work but is penalized by having his social security pension reduced when he does so. When he complains of the inconsistency, he is told that the penalty must accompany the encouragement in order to keep the social security fund fiscally sound.

We now call for increased hiring of disadvantaged youths and at the same time mandate increases in the minimum cost of doing so in order that the youths shall not take jobs from older unionized workers.

The seemingly intractable problems in our economy relating to employment (and other issues) are not likely to be solved by increased push-pull government participation. I am afraid that such increased participation would be a major consequence of the proposed "new directions for a public-private partnership," and it is for that reason I disapprove of the statement.

Page 20, by W. D. EBERLE, *with which* CHARLES KELLER, JR. *and* CHARLES B. STAUFFACHER *have asked to be associated*

This recommendation misses the key point—more study is not needed, as the estimates of the magnitude of illegal aliens are so large, taken together with the new illegal alien flow, that a policy of action is needed promptly if more jobs are to be available. The present and past two Presidential Administrations have collected substantial background information and material both as to the nature and the magnitude of the problem and possible solutions. The longer laws go unenforced, you either get a breakdown, through violating more laws, or an overreaction, through new laws to correct the problem. The illegal alien problem involves not only jobs but the rights of people, foreign policy as to our neighbors, and realism as to enforcement. It seems to me that CED should have urged prompt policy action by the President and Congress to (1) adopt a policy as to future illegal aliens entering the United States, with consideration of enlarging the quotas from certain nations but providing for return of new illegal aliens who enter after a certain date; (2) provide for a secure social security card with strict enforcement by employers for employment; (3) a program to make the adjustment to the new policy as is reasonable and appropriate.

This is not an easy action program, as it involves foreign policy, jobs, and civil rights. But postponing prompt action for such a sizable problem will only create justified increased discontent in our democratic society.

Page 41, by FRAZAR B. WILDE, *with which* ROBERT B. SEMPLE *has asked to be associated*

From the employer's standpoint, it would be helpful if there were a single point of contact with the many programs in existence now and those proposed. It is counterproductive to business and industry and therefore to the employment of disadvantaged groups when employers must coordinate many programs with several groups who are concerned only with their own clientele. A United Way or Combined Health Appeal of these groups would be helpful.

Page 50, by ROBERT R. NATHAN

If there are to be any exemptions from minimum wages, there should be experiments with alternatives rather than adopting exemptions without reasonably clear understanding of the consequences. Theoretically, minimum wage levels might price some inexperienced youngsters out of the market. But there are definite costs and dangers involved. Subminimum pay for young people may well serve to transfer jobs from workers at other age levels to those whom employers can hire for less than the minimum standard. Analyses of this issue are not very encouraging with respect to sizable additions to total employment that might result from minimum wage exemptions.

The erosion in the setting of minimum wage standards could, over time, be very costly. Perhaps many who favor exemptions would, in essence, like to discard the whole concept of minimum wages. Until there is convincing evidence that the net addition to employment is significant and outweighs the undermining of reasonable labor standards, we should not tinker with this measure. The burden of anti-inflation efforts and of stimulating jobs should not be put primarily on the backs of those least able to bear that burden. The less skilled young people and minorities want and need to work. But our society ought to be able to provide them with jobs without resorting to substandard pay. We ought to be able to fight inflation successfully without focusing primarily on those at the bottom of the pay scale.

Another consideration is the likely distortion among industries and employers within industries deriving from paying different wages for similar work. If the marketplace were to function effectively, employers would tend to displace present employees at minimum wage levels with those in the exempted category. The resulting shifts and bitterness can be far more costly than the claimed benefits of those favoring exemptions.

Page 51, by JAMES T. HILL, JR., *with which* G. BARRON MALLORY *and* ROBERT B. SEMPLE *have asked to be associated*

I would favor the total elimination of penalties on social security benefits by reason of earned (i.e., employment) income during the period between age 65 and age 72. It seems to me difficult, if not impossible, to justify the current distinction between investment income (in whatever form), which involves no penalties, and the penalty currently imposed on earned income during the period between age 65 and age 72. The appropriateness of the elimination of the penalty seems to me to be strongly reinforced by the present movement to lift the mandatory retirement age to 70 in the interest of at least partially mitigating current age discrimination policies. In short, I do not believe our recommendations go far enough in this area or adequately address the grave inequity to which I have adverted.

Page 60, by FRANCIS E. FERGUSON

I do believe that this is more than a stereotype and is dismissed too lightly in the policy statement.

Page 65, by FRANCIS E. FERGUSON

I buy this as part of it, but far more central in my opinion is a return to plain basic education in our public and private schools, to readin', writin' and 'rithmetic.

Page 66, by FRANCIS E. FERGUSON

Our experience is not as favorable as indicated here.

Page 82, by CHARLES KELLER, JR.

I hope the importance of Chapter 6 will not be overlooked because it comes last in the statement. The United States has no effective national labor exchange, and it is essential that ES be reorganized to provide this essential service. I would go further than the policy statement suggests and urge the removal of ES from state control and its merger with CETA. The steps suggested in Chapter 6 are the minimum required.

Appendix Table 1. Comparison of Major Unemployment Indicators, 1965, 1973, and 1976

Selected Categories	Number of Unemployed (thousands)		
	1965	1973	1976
Total, 16 and over	3,366	4,304	7,302
Both sexes, 16 to 19	874	1,225	1,701
Both sexes, 20 to 24	557	985	1,670
Men, 25 and over	1,109	1,076	2,131
Women, 25 and over	809	1,016	1,799
White	2,691	3,411	5,871
Black and others	676	894	1,432
Nonwhite, 16 to 19	169	275	345
Household heads	1,257	1,471	2,763
Married men with spouse	883	905	1,687
Full-time workers	2,791	3,291	5,874
Part-time workers	575	1,013	1,414

Sources: Department of Labor, *Employment and Training Report of the President*, 1977; and *Employment and Earnings* (various issues).

Unemployment Rate (percent)			Percent of Total Labor Force			Percent of Total Unemployed		
965	1973	1976	1965	1973	1976	1965	1973	1976
4.5	4.9	7.7	100.0	100.0	100.0	100.0	100.0	100.0
14.8	14.5	19.0	7.9	9.5	9.4	26.2	28.5	23.3
6.7	7.8	12.0	11.1	14.3	14.7	16.6	22.9	22.9
2.8	2.5	4.9	53.7	47.9	46.3	33.1	25.0	29.2
4.0	4.1	6.4	27.3	28.3	29.5	24.1	23.6	24.6
4.1	4.3	7.0	88.8	88.7	88.5	79.9	79.2	80.4
8.1	8.9	13.1	11.2	11.3	11.5	20.1	20.8	19.6
26.2	30.2	37.1	0.9	1.0	1.0	5.1	6.4	4.7
2.7	2.9	5.1	62.5	57.2	57.2	37.3	34.2	37.9
2.4	2.3	4.2	49.4	44.4	42.4	26.2	21.0	23.1
4.2	4.3	7.3	88.5	85.5	85.3	82.9	76.5	80.6
6.7	7.9	10.1	11.5	14.5	14.7	17.1	23.5	19.4

Table 2. Total Population, by Age and Sex (*millions*)

Age	Actual				Projected	
	1960	1970	1975	1980	1985	1990
Both sexes						
16 years and over	121.8	141.1	153.6	165.3	174.0	181.1
16 to 19 years	10.7	15.2	16.6	16.6	14.2	13.4
20 to 24 years	11.1	17.1	19.1	20.8	20.4	17.8
25 to 44 years	47.1	48.1	53.4	61.4	70.6	77.0
45 to 54 years	20.6	23.1	23.6	22.5	22.2	25.0
55 to 64 years	15.6	18.5	19.5	20.8	21.2	20.3
65 years and over	16.7	19.1	21.3	23.3	25.3	27.5
Males						
16 years and over	59.4	67.7	73.6	79.1	83.1	86.4
16 to 19 years	5.4	7.7	8.4	8.4	7.2	6.8
20 to 24 years	5.6	8.6	9.6	10.4	10.2	8.9
25 to 44 years	23.2	23.6	26.2	30.2	34.7	37.9
45 to 54 years	10.1	11.1	11.4	10.9	10.8	12.2
55 to 64 years	7.6	8.7	9.2	9.8	10.0	9.6
65 years and over	7.5	8.0	8.8	9.5	10.2	11.0
Females						
16 years and over	62.4	73.3	80.0	86.2	90.9	94.7
16 to 19 years	5.3	7.5	8.2	8.2	7.0	6.6
20 to 24 years	5.5	8.5	9.5	10.4	10.2	8.9
25 to 44 years	23.9	24.5	27.2	31.2	35.9	39.1
45 to 54 years	10.4	12.0	12.2	11.6	11.4	12.9
55 to 64 years	8.1	9.8	10.3	11.0	11.2	10.7
65 years and over	9.1	11.1	12.5	13.8	15.1	16.5

Source: Bureau of Labor Statistics, *Special Labor Force Projections to 1990*, Special Labor Force Report 197.

Table 3. Percent Distribution of Total Labor Force, by Age and Sex

Age	Actual				Projected	
	1960	1970	1975	1980	1985	1990
Both sexes						
16 years and over	100.0	100.0	100.0	100.0	100.0	100.0
16 to 19 years	7.2	8.9	9.7	9.1	7.5	6.9
20 to 24 years	10.6	14.3	15.1	15.4	14.4	12.2
25 to 44 years	44.0	40.1	42.2	45.2	49.7	52.4
45 to 54 years	20.7	19.8	18.1	15.9	14.9	16.2
55 to 64 years	13.0	13.1	11.8	11.5	10.8	9.7
65 years and over	4.4	3.7	3.1	2.9	2.7	2.7
Males						
16 years and over	67.7	63.3	60.8	59.7	58.6	58.0
16 to 19 years	4.4	5.1	5.4	5.0	4.1	3.7
20 to 24 years	7.1	8.6	8.6	8.5	7.7	6.4
25 to 44 years	30.9	26.5	26.4	27.8	29.9	31.0
45 to 54 years	13.4	12.2	11.0	9.6	8.8	9.4
55 to 64 years	8.9	8.3	7.4	7.0	6.4	5.8
65 years and over	3.2	2.5	2.0	1.8	1.7	1.6
Females						
16 years and over	32.3	36.7	39.1	40.3	41.4	42.0
16 to 19 years	2.9	3.8	4.3	4.1	3.4	3.2
20 to 24 years	3.6	5.7	6.4	6.9	6.7	5.8
25 to 44 years	13.1	13.6	15.8	17.4	19.8	21.4
45 to 54 years	7.3	7.6	7.0	6.4	6.1	6.7
55 to 64 years	4.1	4.8	4.5	4.4	4.3	3.9
65 years and over	1.3	1.2	1.1	1.1	1.1	1.1

Source: Bureau of Labor Statistics, *New Labor Force Projections to 1990*, Special Labor Force Report 197.

Table 4. Total Labor Force, by Age and Sex (*millions*)

Age	Actual					Projected	
	1950	1960	1970	1975	1980	1985	1990
Both sexes							
16 years and over	63.9	72.1	85.9	94.8	103.8	110.7	115.9
16 to 19 years	4.5	5.2	7.6	9.2	9.4	8.3	8.0
20 to 24 years	7.9	7.7	12.3	14.3	16.0	16.0	14.2
25 to 44 years	29.3	31.7	34.5	40.0	46.9	55.0	60.7
45 to 54 years	11.5	14.9	17.0	17.1	16.5	16.5	18.7
55 to 64 years	7.6	9.4	11.3	11.2	11.9	11.9	11.2
65 years and over	3.0	3.2	3.2	2.9	3.0	3.0	3.1
Males							
16 years and over	45.4	48.9	54.3	57.7	62.0	64.9	67.2
16 to 19 years	2.8	3.2	4.4	5.1	5.2	4.5	4.3
20 to 24 years	5.2	5.1	7.4	8.2	8.9	8.6	7.5
25 to 44 years	21.0	22.3	22.8	25.0	28.8	33.0	35.9
45 to 54 years	8.2	9.6	10.5	10.5	9.9	9.7	10.9
55 to 64 years	5.8	6.4	7.1	7.0	7.3	7.2	6.7
65 years and over	2.5	2.3	2.2	1.9	1.9	1.8	1.9
Females							
16 years and over	18.4	23.3	31.6	37.1	41.8	45.8	48.7
16 to 19 years	1.7	2.1	3.3	4.1	4.2	3.8	3.7
20 to 24 years	2.7	2.6	4.9	6.1	7.1	7.4	6.7
25 to 44 years	8.3	9.4	11.7	15.0	18.1	22.0	24.8
45 to 54 years	3.3	5.3	6.5	6.7	6.6	6.8	7.8
55 to 64 years	1.8	3.0	4.2	4.2	4.6	4.7	4.5
65 years and over	0.6	0.9	1.1	1.0	1.1	1.2	1.3

Source: Bureau of Labor Statistics, *New Labor Force Projections to 1990*, Special Labor Force Report 197.

Table 5. Total Labor Force Participation Rates, by Age and Sex (percent)

Age	Actual				Projected	
	1960	1970	1975	1980	1985	1990
Both sexes						
16 years and over	59.2	60.9	61.7	62.8	63.6	64.0
16 to 19 years	48.9	50.4	55.1	57.3	58.3	59.3
20 to 24 years	67.5	71.8	74.9	77.0	78.5	79.5
25 to 44 years	67.6	71.7	75.0	76.3	77.9	78.8
45 to 54 years	71.5	73.6	72.7	73.6	74.4	74.9
55 to 64 years	60.2	61.1	57.4	57.1	56.0	55.4
65 years and over	20.3	16.9	13.8	12.9	11.9	11.3
Males						
16 years and over	82.4	80.3	78.5	78.4	78.1	77.8
16 to 19 years	58.6	57.3	60.9	62.6	62.7	63.2
20 to 24 years	88.9	86.1	85.7	85.4	84.4	83.6
25 to 44 years	96.4	96.8	95.5	95.4	95.1	94.9
45 to 54 years	94.3	94.2	92.0	91.3	90.6	90.2
55 to 64 years	85.2	81.8	75.7	74.3	71.6	69.9
65 years and over	32.2	26.9	21.7	19.9	18.0	16.8
Females						
16 years and over	37.1	43.0	46.4	48.5	50.4	51.5
16 to 19 years	39.1	43.4	49.2	51.9	53.7	55.3
20 to 24 years	46.1	57.5	64.2	68.6	72.6	75.3
25 to 44 years	39.6	47.6	55.1	57.8	61.2	63.3
45 to 54 years	49.3	54.5	54.6	57.1	59.1	60.5
55 to 64 years	36.7	42.6	41.0	41.9	42.2	42.3
65 years and over	10.5	9.6	8.2	8.1	7.8	7.6

Source: Bureau of Labor Statistics, *Special Labor Force Projections to 1990,* Special Labor Force Report 197.

Objectives of the Committee for Economic Development

For thirty-five years, the Committee for Economic Development has been a respected influence on the formation of business and public policy. CED is devoted to these two objectives:

To develop, through objective research and informed discussion, findings and recommendations for private and public policy which will contribute to preserving and strengthening our free society, achieving steady economic growth at high employment and reasonably stable prices, increasing productivity and living standards, providing greater and more equal opportunity for every citizen, and improving the quality of life for all.

To bring about increasing understanding by present and future leaders in business, government, and education and among concerned citizens of the importance of these objectives and the ways in which they can be achieved.

CED's work is supported strictly by private voluntary contributions from business and industry, foundations, and individuals. It is independent, nonprofit, nonpartisan, and nonpolitical.

The two hundred trustees, who generally are presidents or board chairmen of corporations and presidents of universities, are chosen for their individual capacities rather than as representatives of any particular interests. By working with scholars, they unite business judgment and experience with scholarship in analyzing the issues and developing recommendations to resolve the economic problems that constantly arise in a dynamic and democratic society.

Through this business-academic partnership, CED endeavors to develop policy statements and other research materials that commend themselves as guides to public and business policy; for use as texts in college economics and political science courses and in management training courses; for consideration and discussion by newspaper and magazine editors, columnists, and commentators; and for distribution abroad to promote better understanding of the American economic system.

CED believes that by enabling businessmen to demonstrate constructively their concern for the general welfare, it is helping business to earn and maintain the national and community respect essential to the successful functioning of the free enterprise capitalist system.

Statements on National Policy
Issued by the Research and Policy Committee
(publications in print)

Social Responsibilities of Business Corporations *(June 1971)*

Education for the Urban Disadvantaged:
  From Preschool to Employment *(March 1971)*

Further Weapons Against Inflation *(November 1970)*

Making Congress More Effective *(September 1970)*

Training and Jobs for the Urban Poor *(July 1970)*

Improving the Public Welfare System *(April 1970)*

Reshaping Government in Metropolitan Areas *(February 1970)*

Economic Growth in the United States *(October 1969)*

Assisting Development in Low-Income Countries *(September 1969)*

*Nontariff Distortions of Trade *(September 1969)*

Fiscal and Monetary Policies for Steady Economic Growth *(January 1969)*

Financing a Better Election System *(December 1968)*

Innovation in Education: New Directions for the American School *(July 1968)*

Modernizing State Government *(July 1967)*

*Trade Policy Toward Low-Income Countries *(June 1967)*

How Low Income Countries Can Advance Their Own Growth *(September 1966)*

Modernizing Local Government *(July 1966)*

Budgeting for National Objectives *(January 1966)*

Educating Tomorrow's Managers *(October 1964)*

Improving Executive Management in the Federal Government *(July 1964)*

Economic Literacy for Americans *(March 1962)*

---

*Statements issued in association with CED counterpart organizations in foreign countries.

Close relationships exist between the Committee for Economic Development and independent, nonpolitical research organizations in other countries. Such counterpart groups are composed of business executives and scholars and have objectives similar to those of CED, which they pursue by similarly objective methods. CED cooperates with these organizations on research and study projects of common interest to the various countries concerned. This program has resulted in a number of joint policy statements involving such international matters as East-West trade, assistance to the developing countries, and the reduction of nontariff barriers to trade.

CEDA Committee for Economic Development of Australia
139 Macquarie Street, Sydney 2001,
New South Wales, Australia

CEPES Europäische Vereinigung für
Wirtschaftliche und Soziale Entwicklung
Reuterweg 14, 6000 Frankfurt/Main, West Germany

IDEP Institut de l'Entreprise
6, rue Clément-Marot, 75008 Paris, France

経済同友会 Keizai Doyukai
(Japan Committee for Economic Development)
Japan Industrial Club Bldg.
1 Marunouchi, Chiyoda-ku, Tokyo, Japan

PEP Political and Economic Planning
12 Upper Belgrave Street, London, SWIX 8BB, England

SNS Studieförbundet Näringsliv och Samhälle
Sköldungagatan, 2, 11427 Stockholm, Sweden